The Adventure of ODD Head + A Box of Outrageous

by Marcellous Lovelace
(Art Book)

The Adventure of ODD Head + A Box of Outrageous
An art book by Marcellous Lovelace

Written and drawn in Phoenix Arizona at Work at
Cholla Public Library during down time.
Contact www.marcellouslovelace.com

I create Art to escape colonial oppression
My ideas are my own independent escape

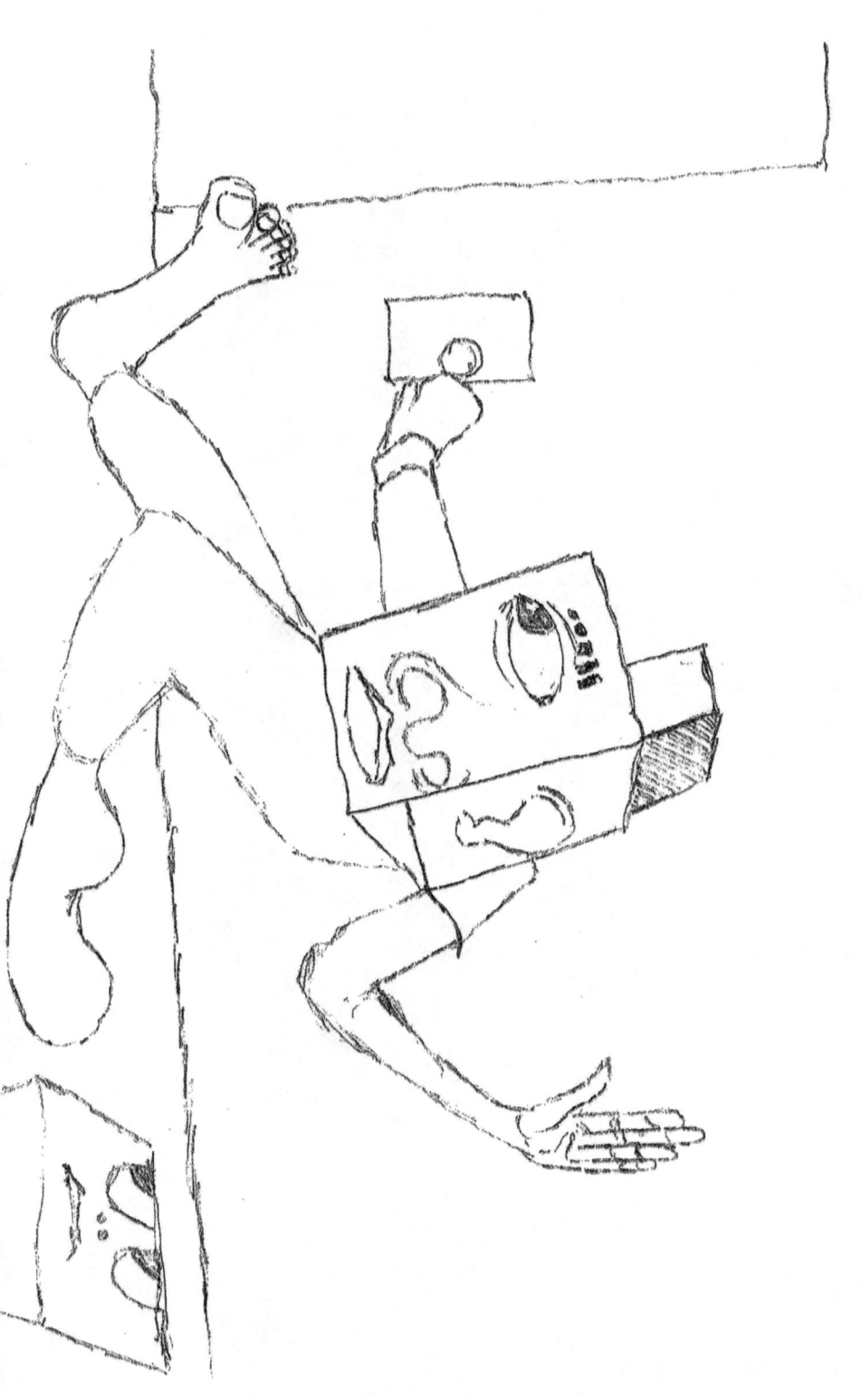

I draw sketches to pass see my thoughts

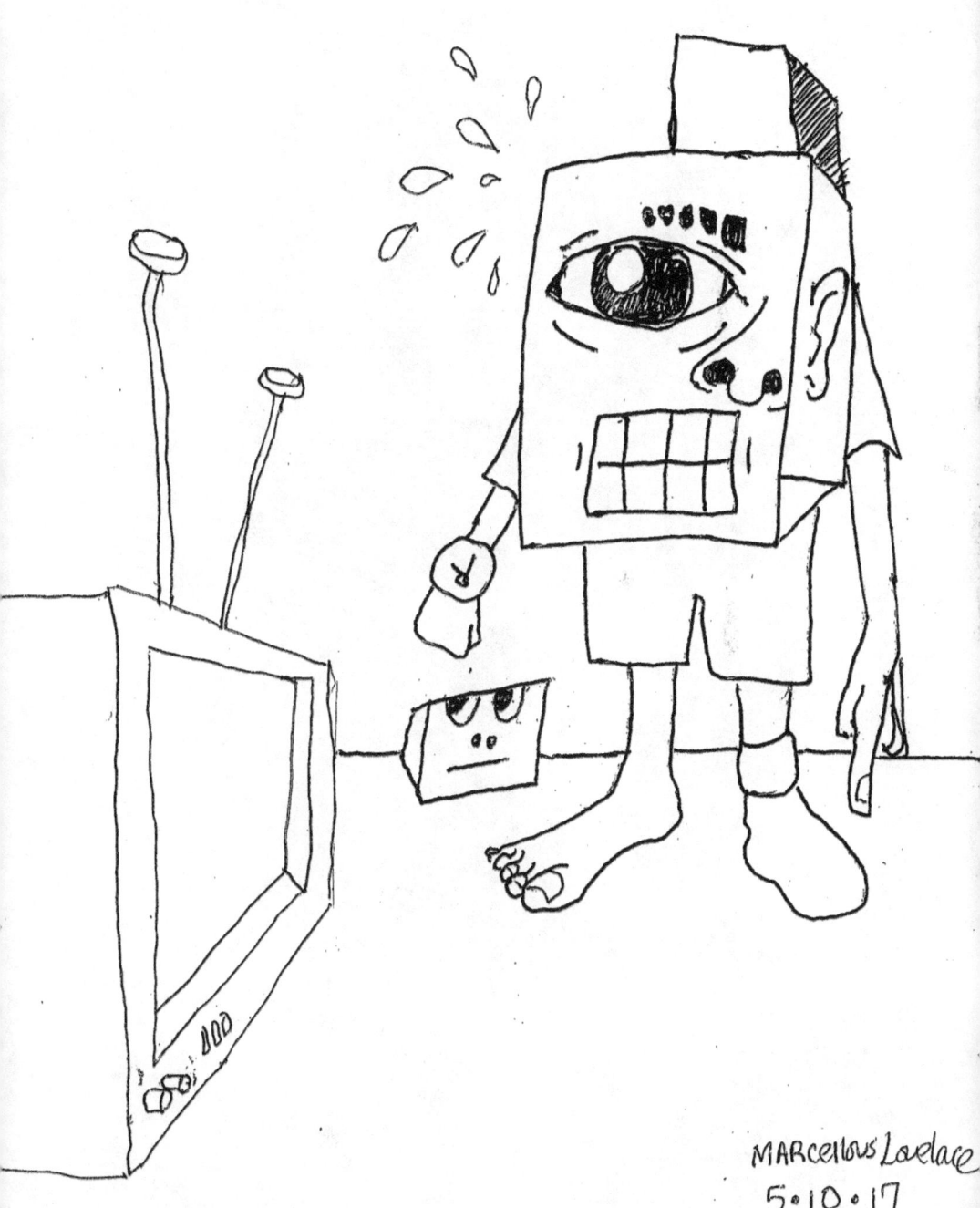

MARCellous Lovelace
5·10·17

My dreams are to only be myself

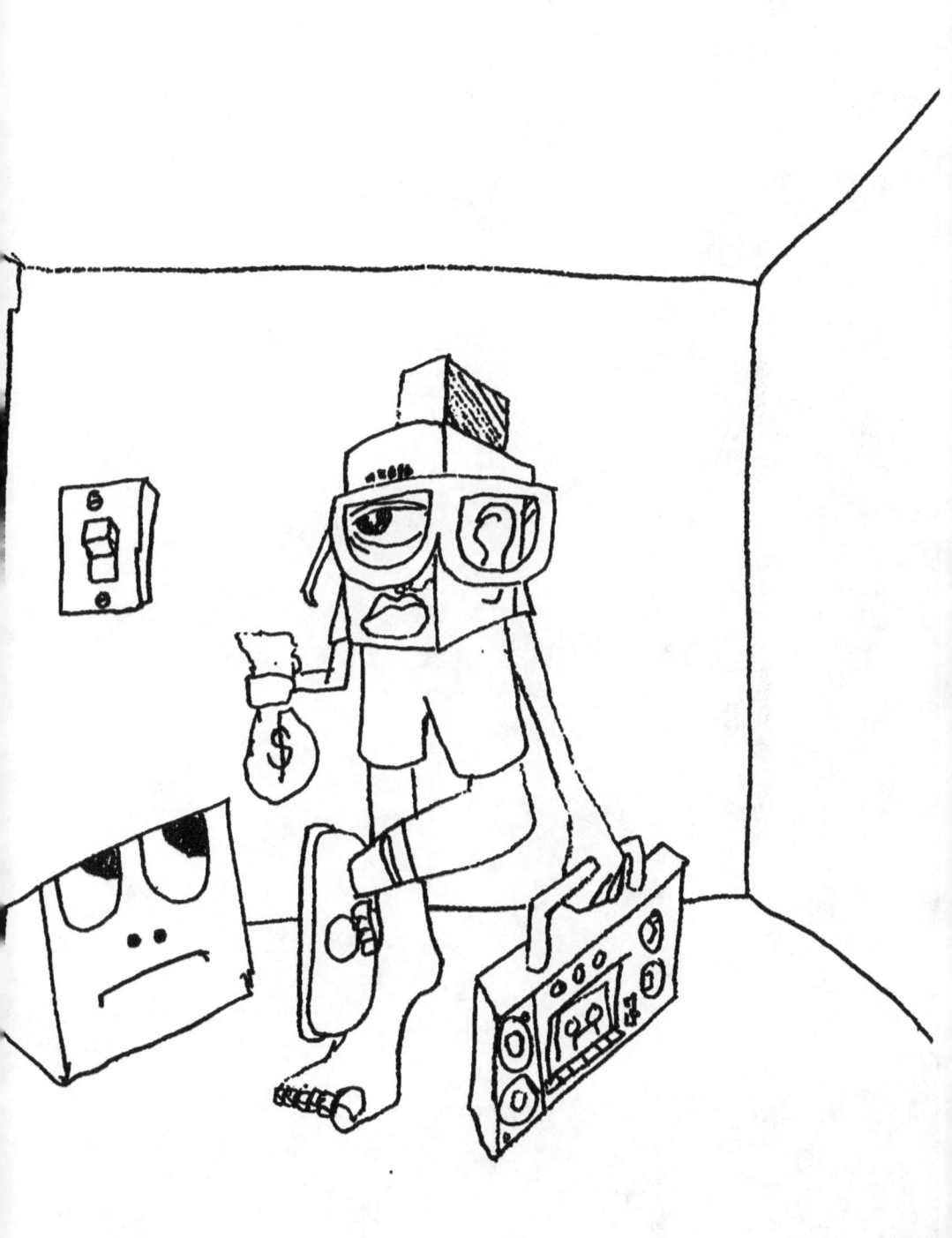

They want my voice but can't hear me

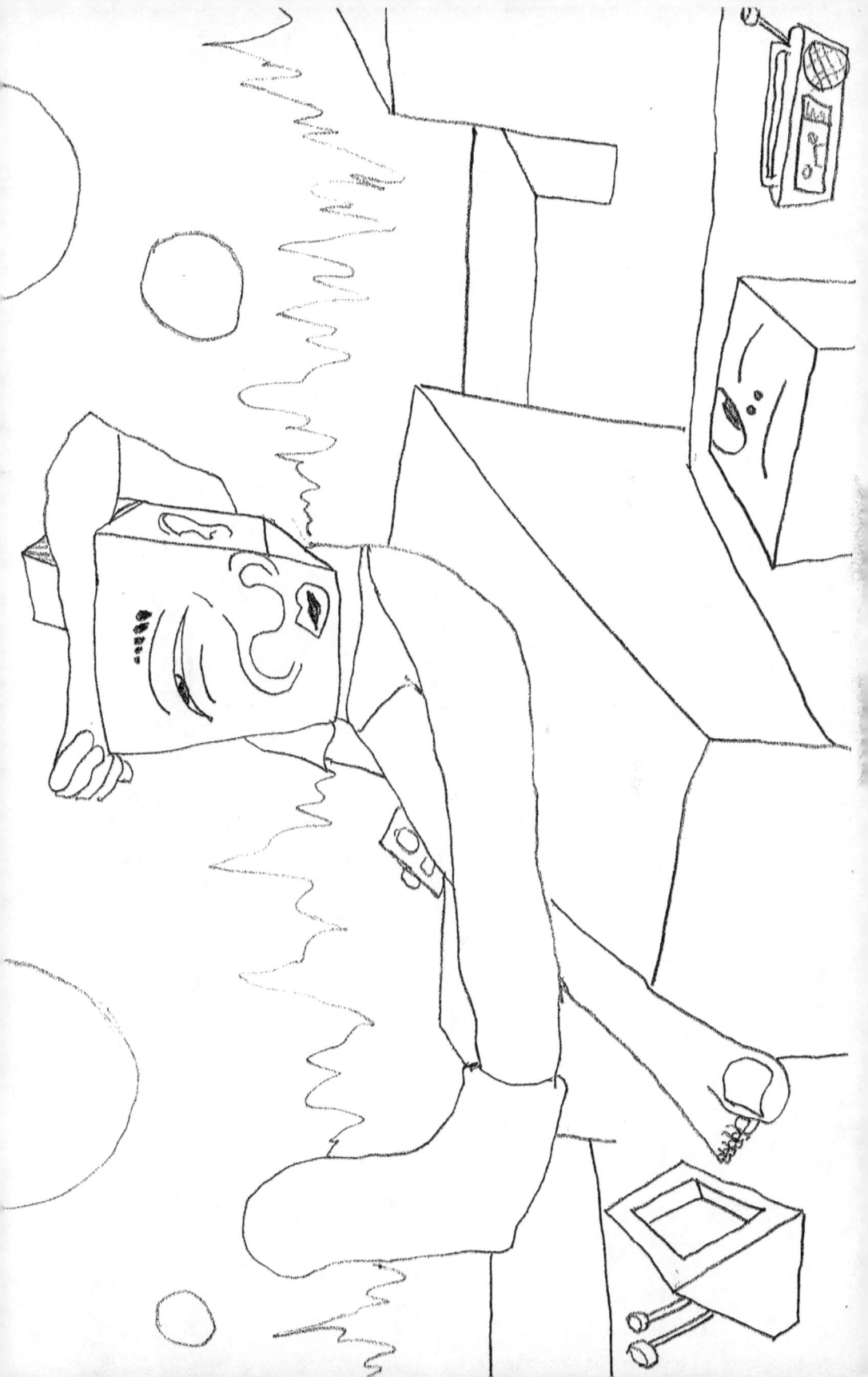

I radiate creation

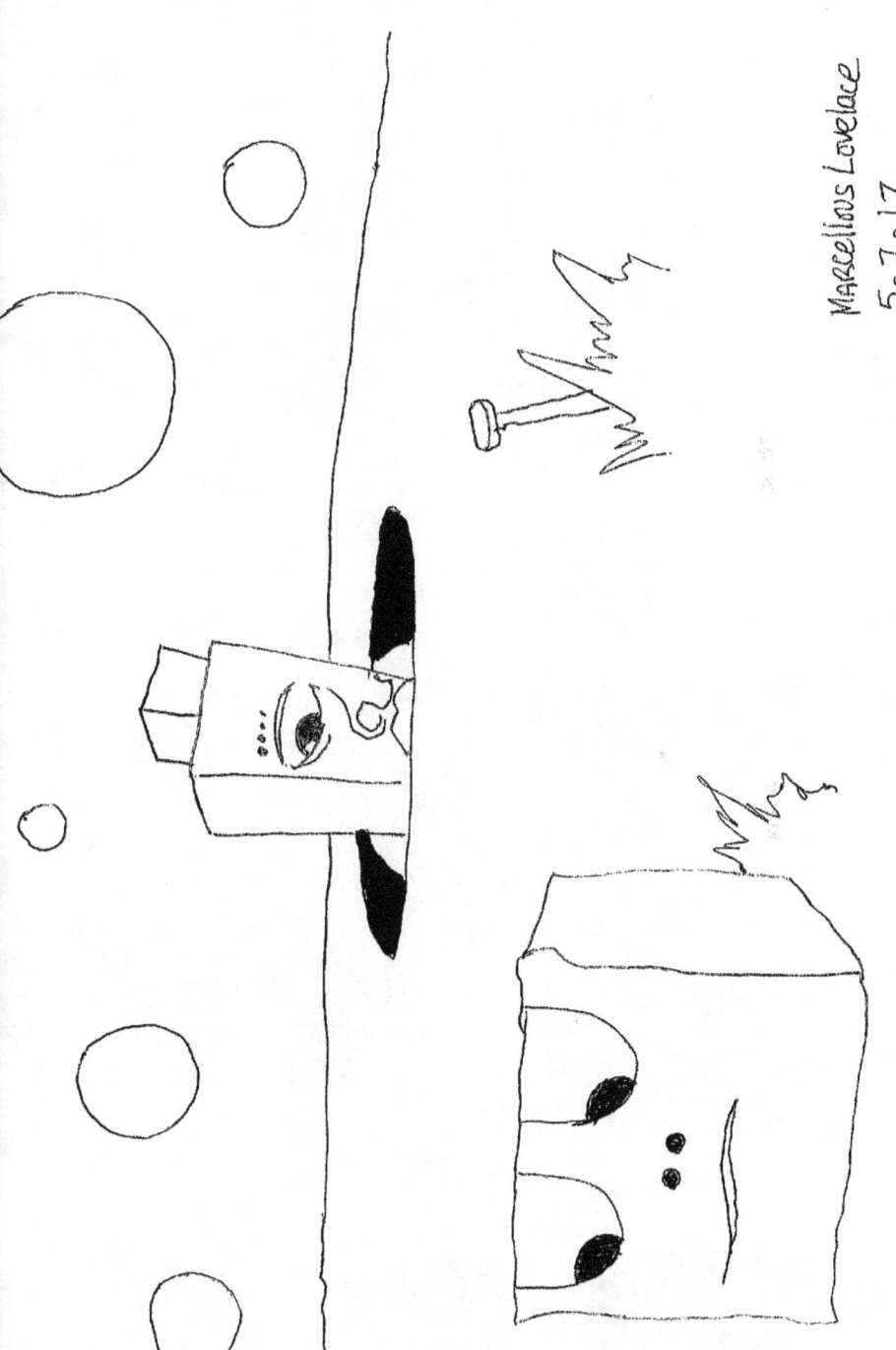

Marcelious Lovelace
5·7·17

At work I think of peace

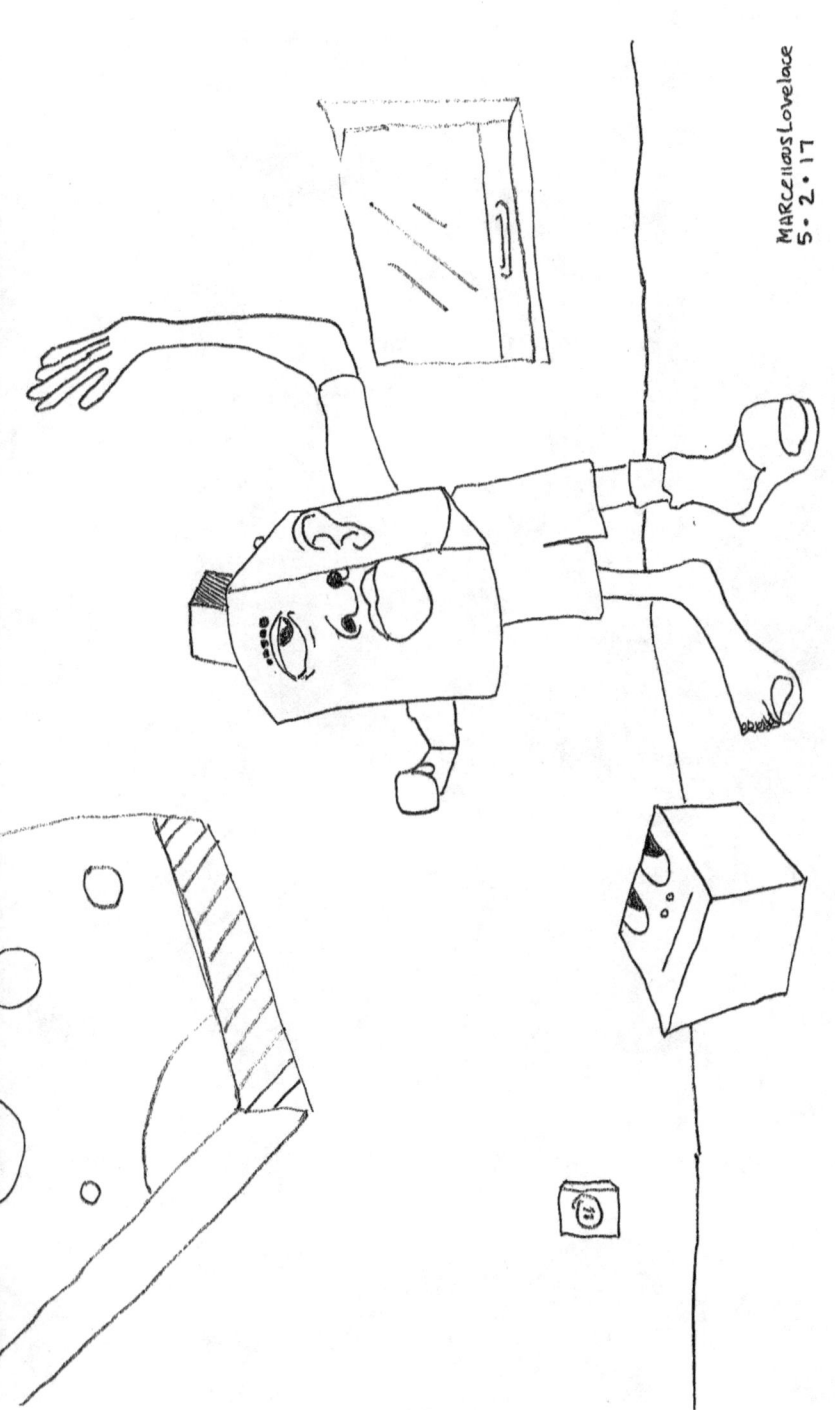

Growth through struggle

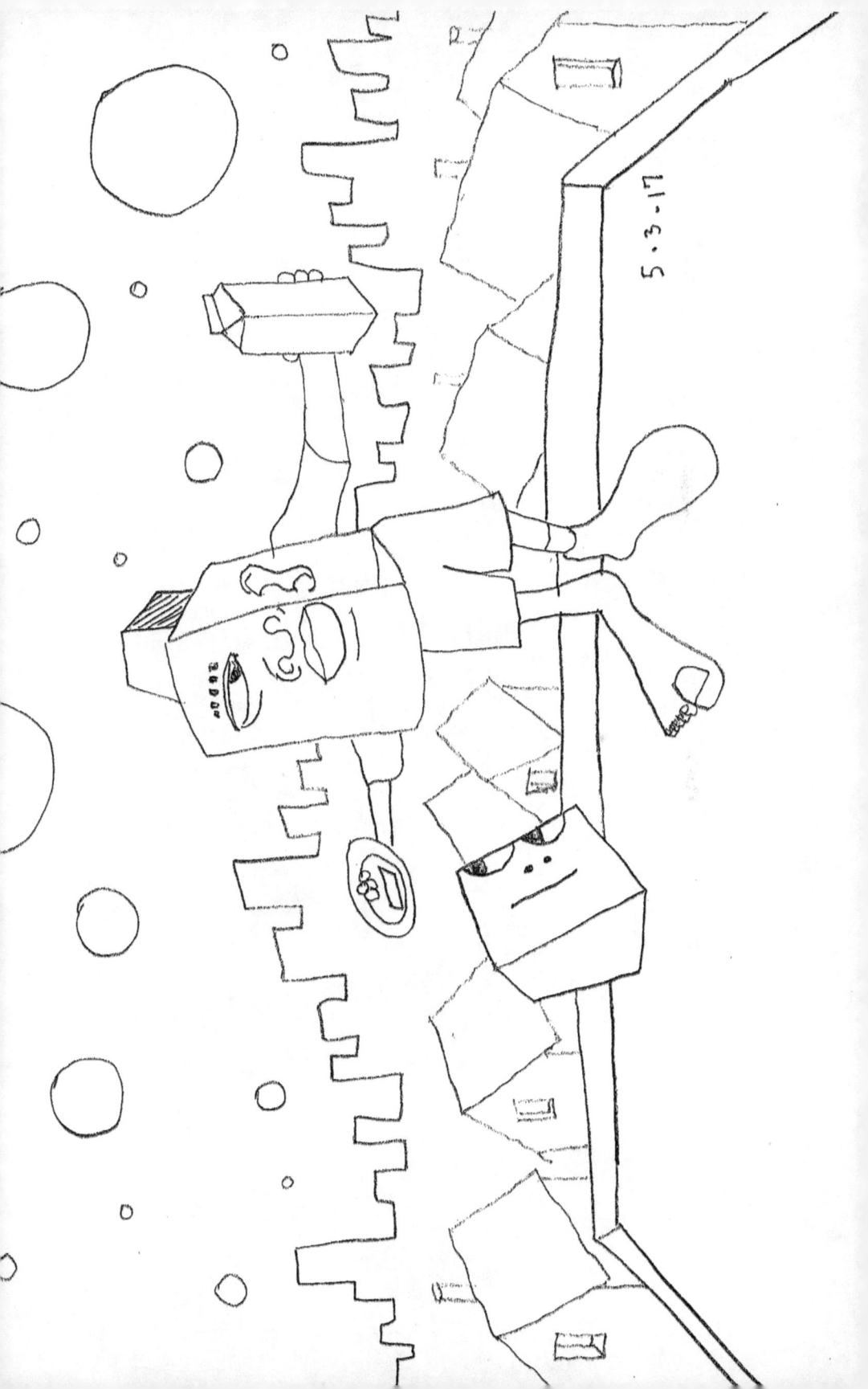

Pain is not bringing us closer

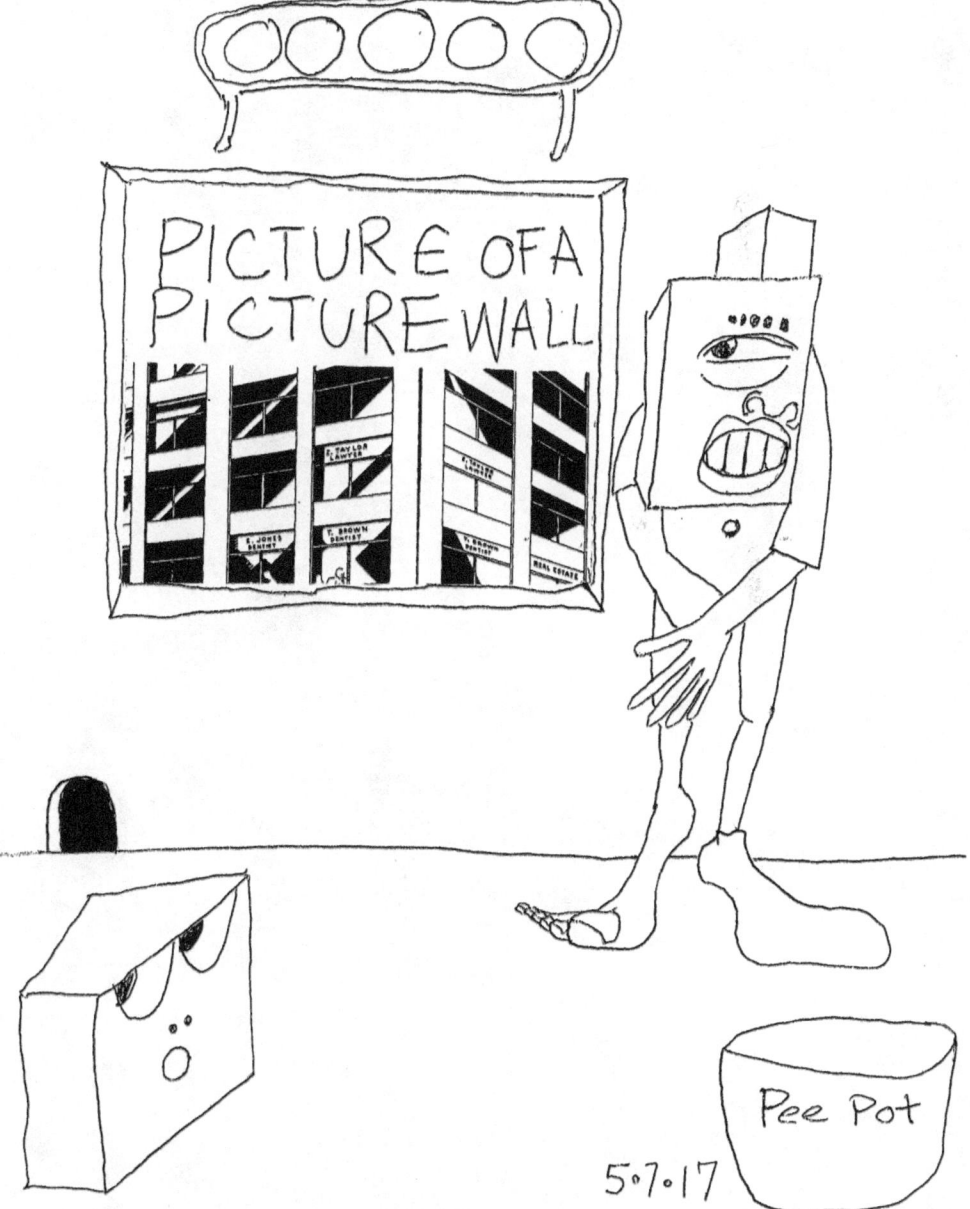

We are unwelcome citizens

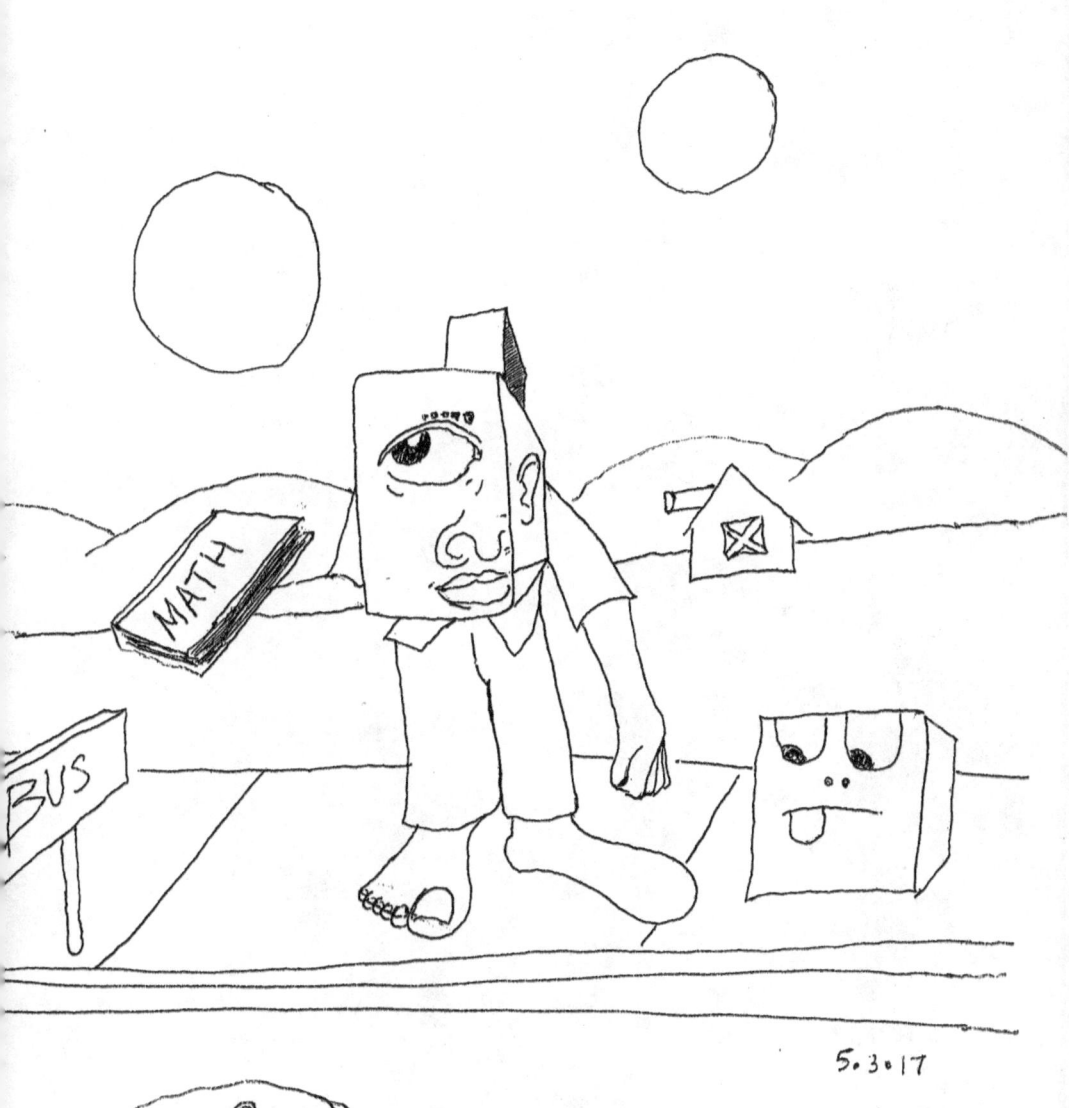

5.3.17

Only I can see my future

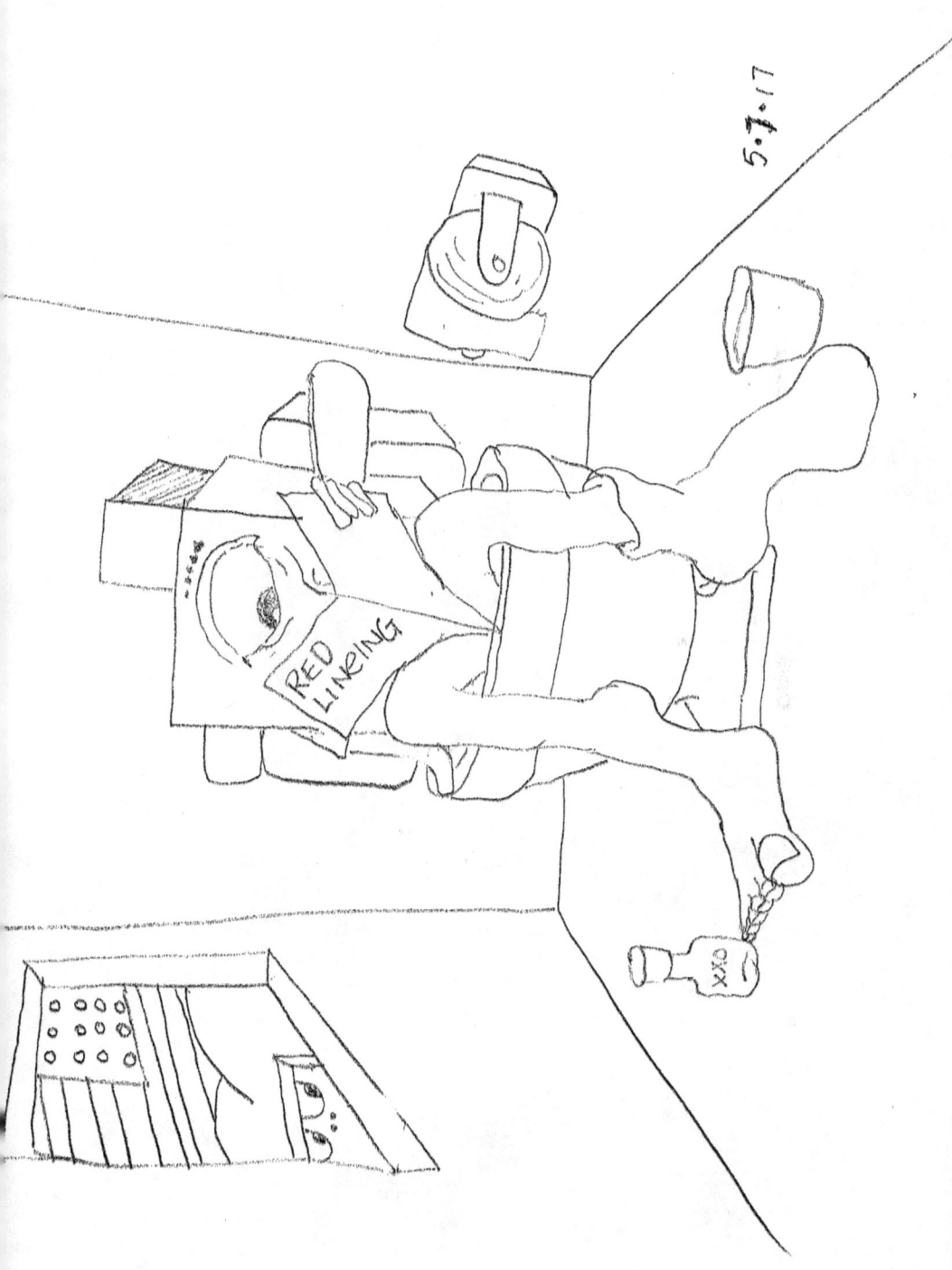

I feel like the Male Characters in Spike Lee films: Malcolm X Da Sweet Blood of Jesus X She Hate Me ...

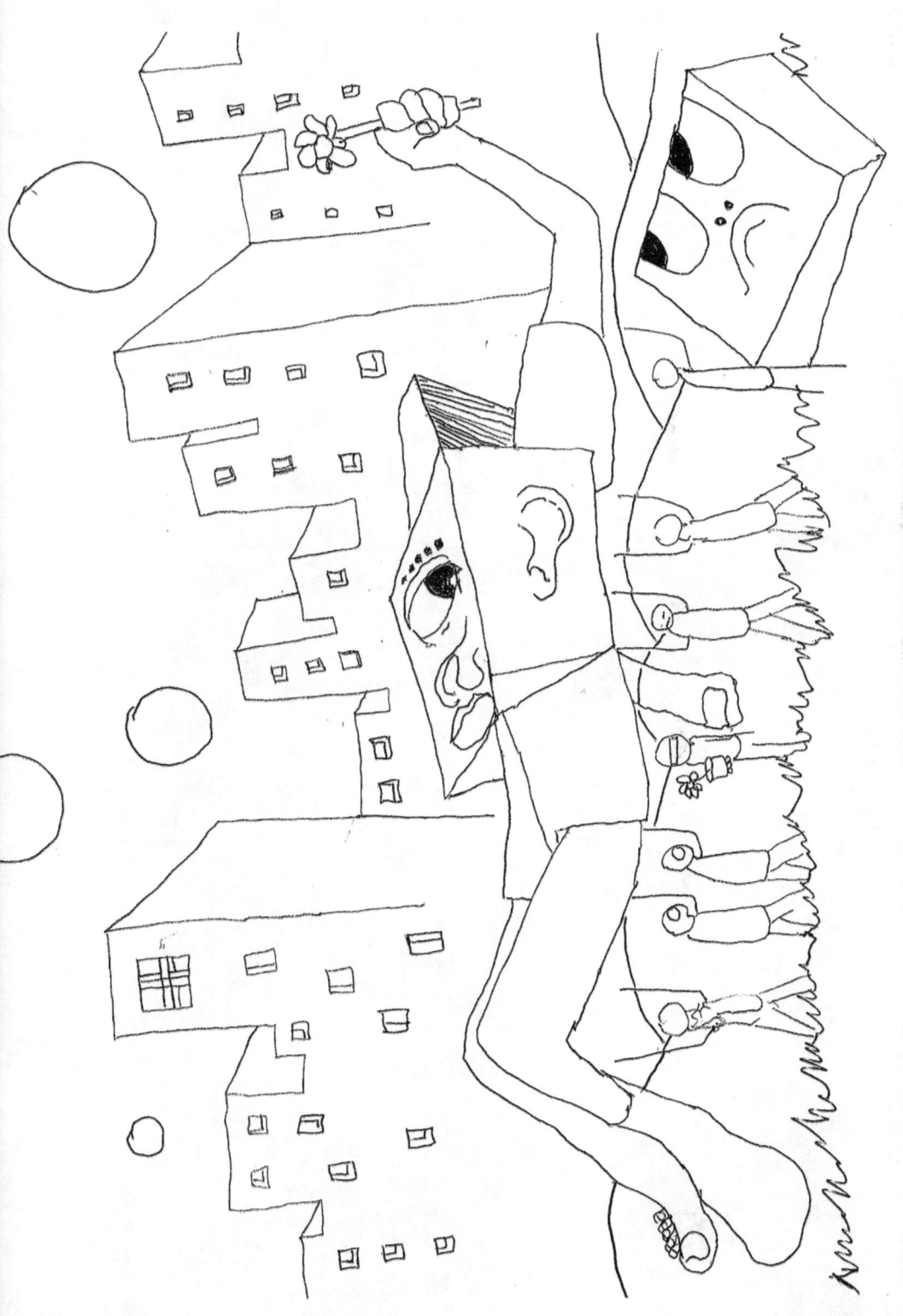

The Idea of Uniqueness

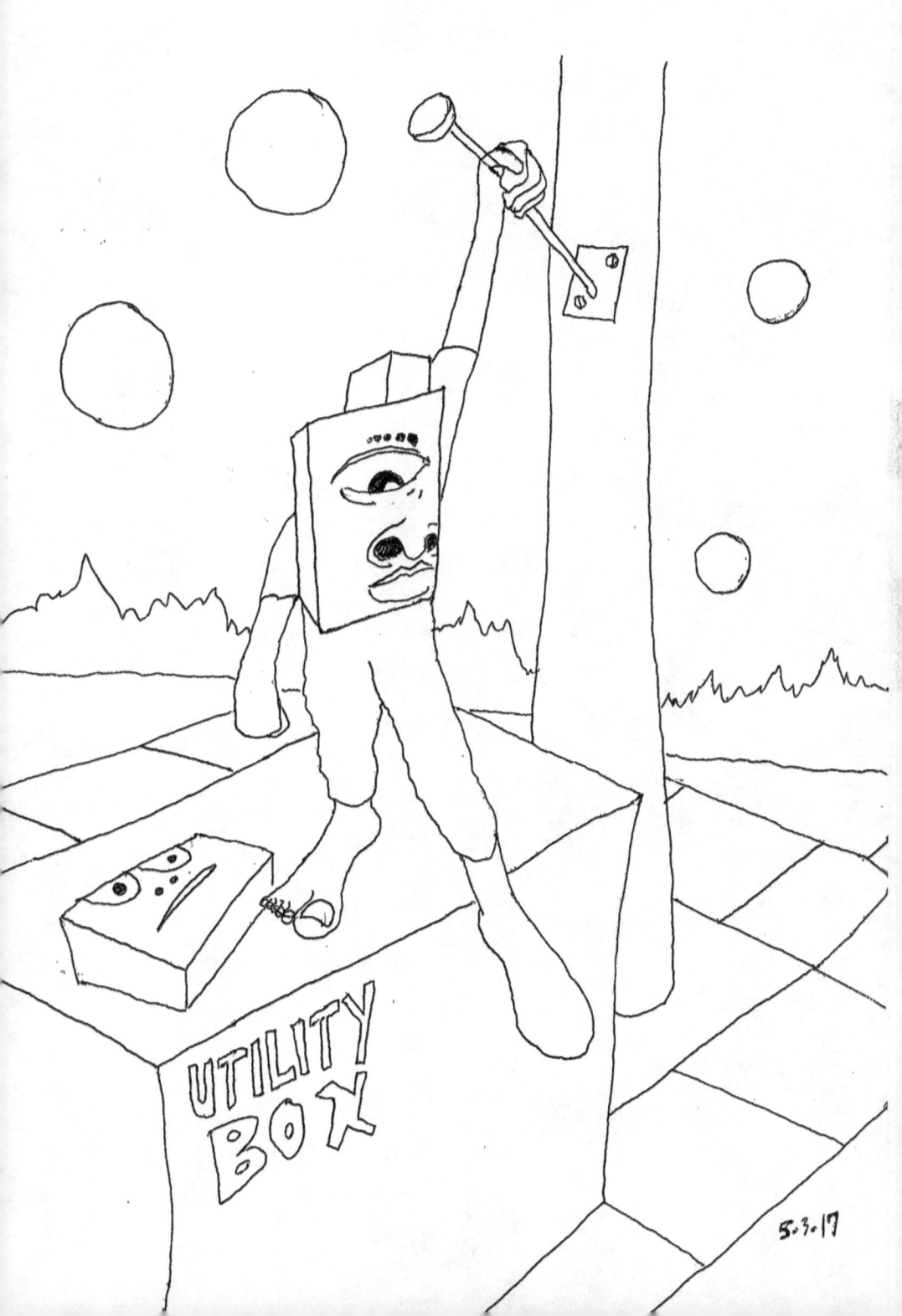

UTILITY
BOX

5·3·17

Broken in parts my heart still sees what she desires but what I don't have to give!

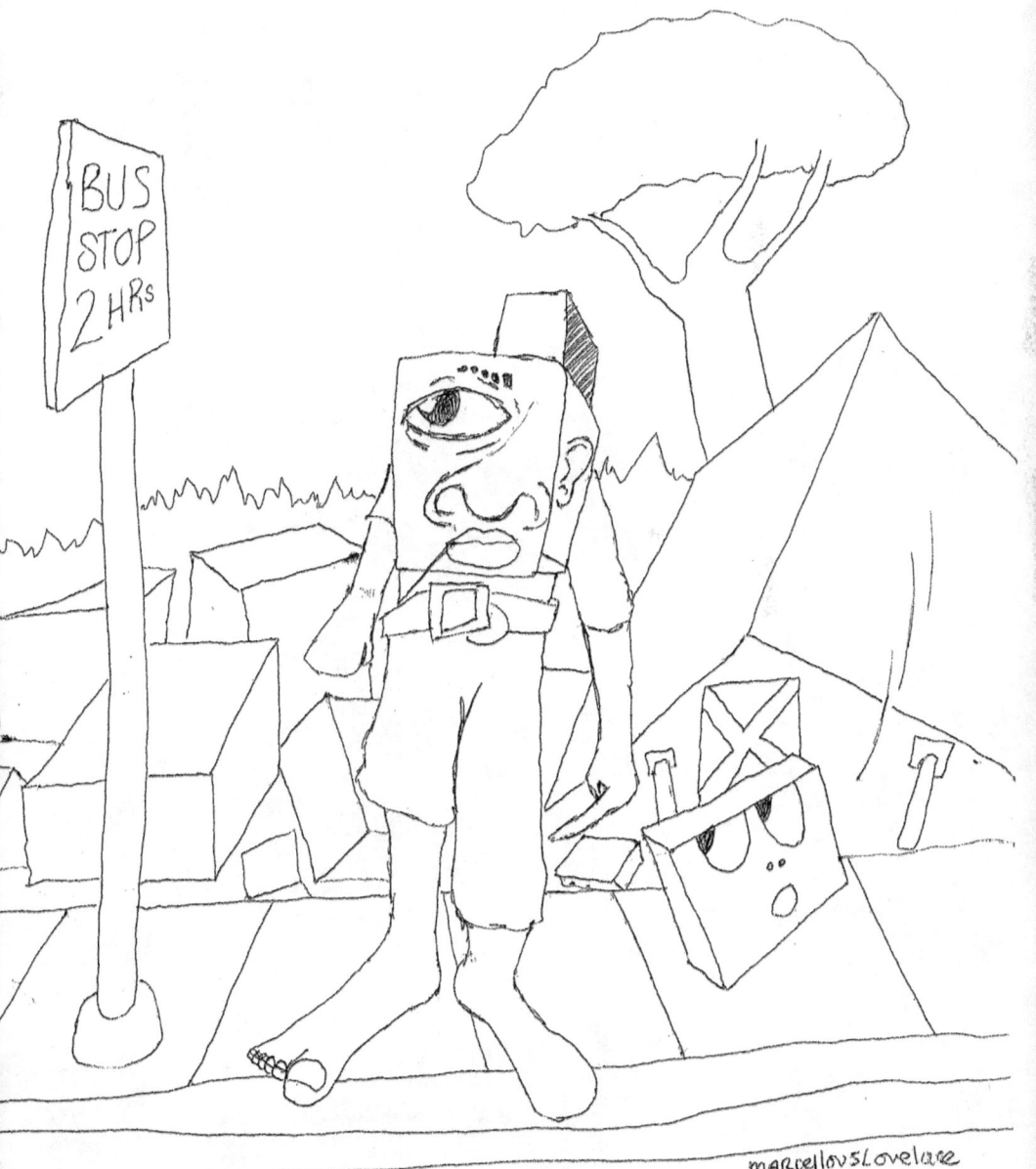

Using voices

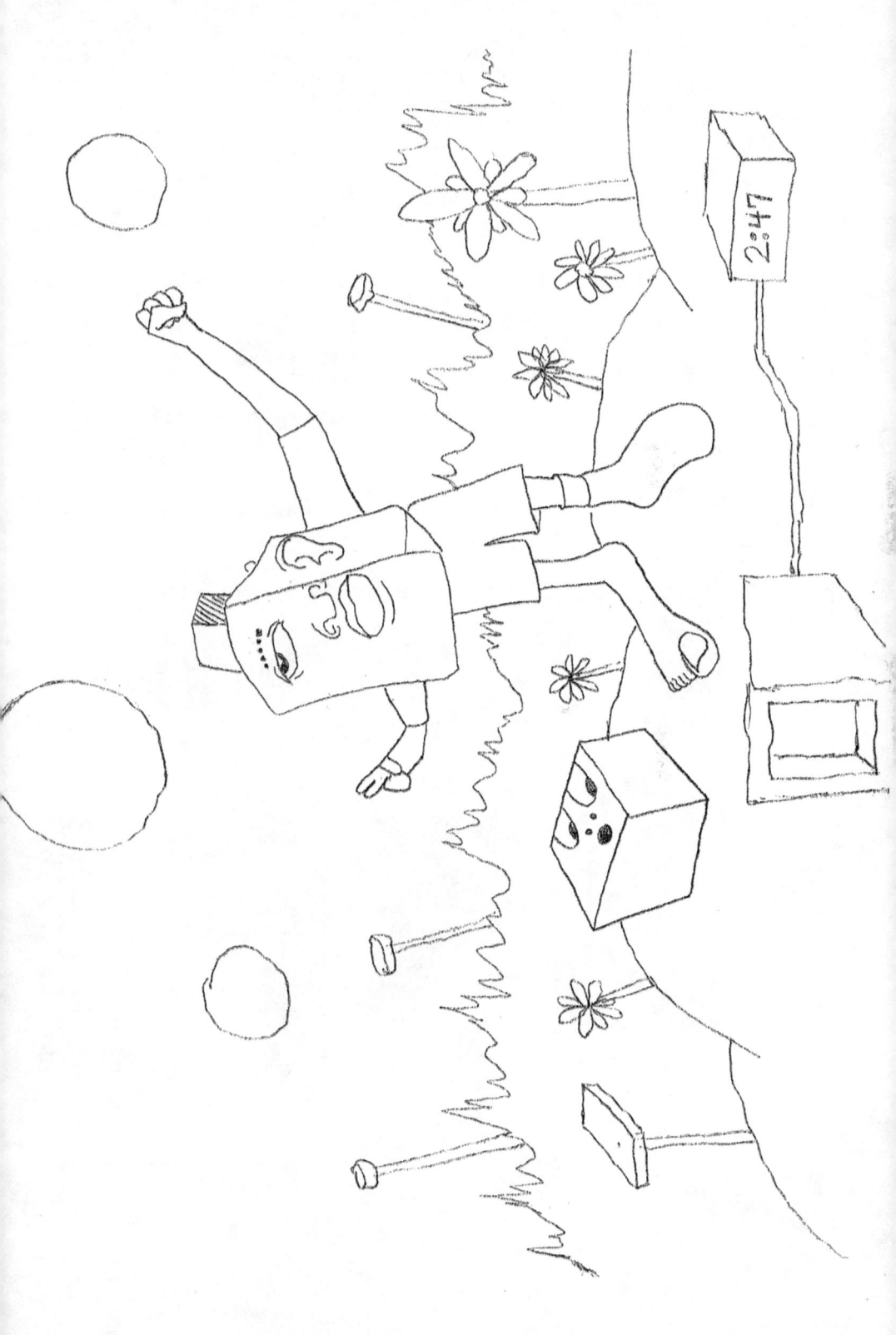

It's no one like you

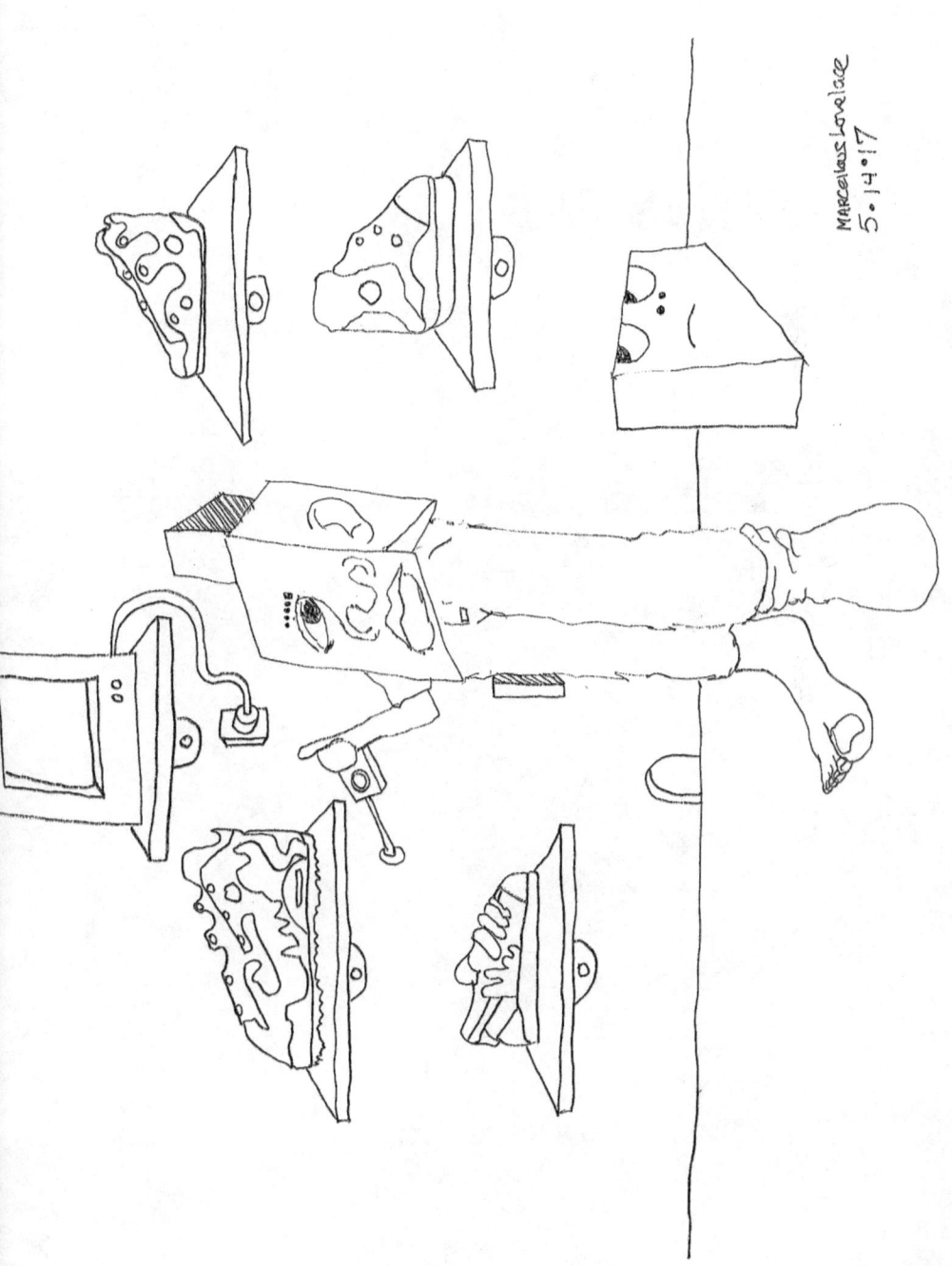

Marcellous Lovelace
5·14·17

They say we are special

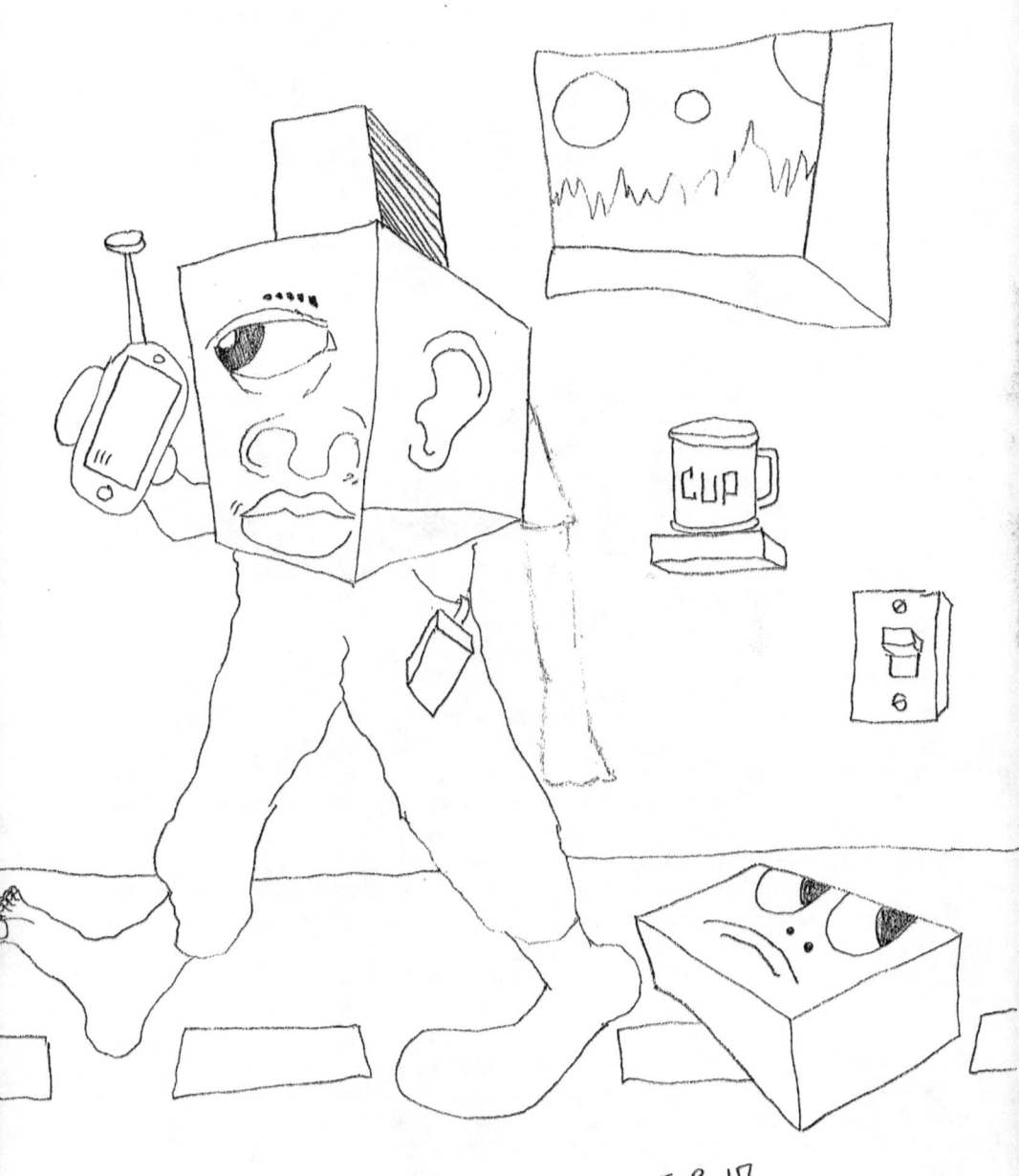

CUP

5·9·17

Art to escape yesterday now

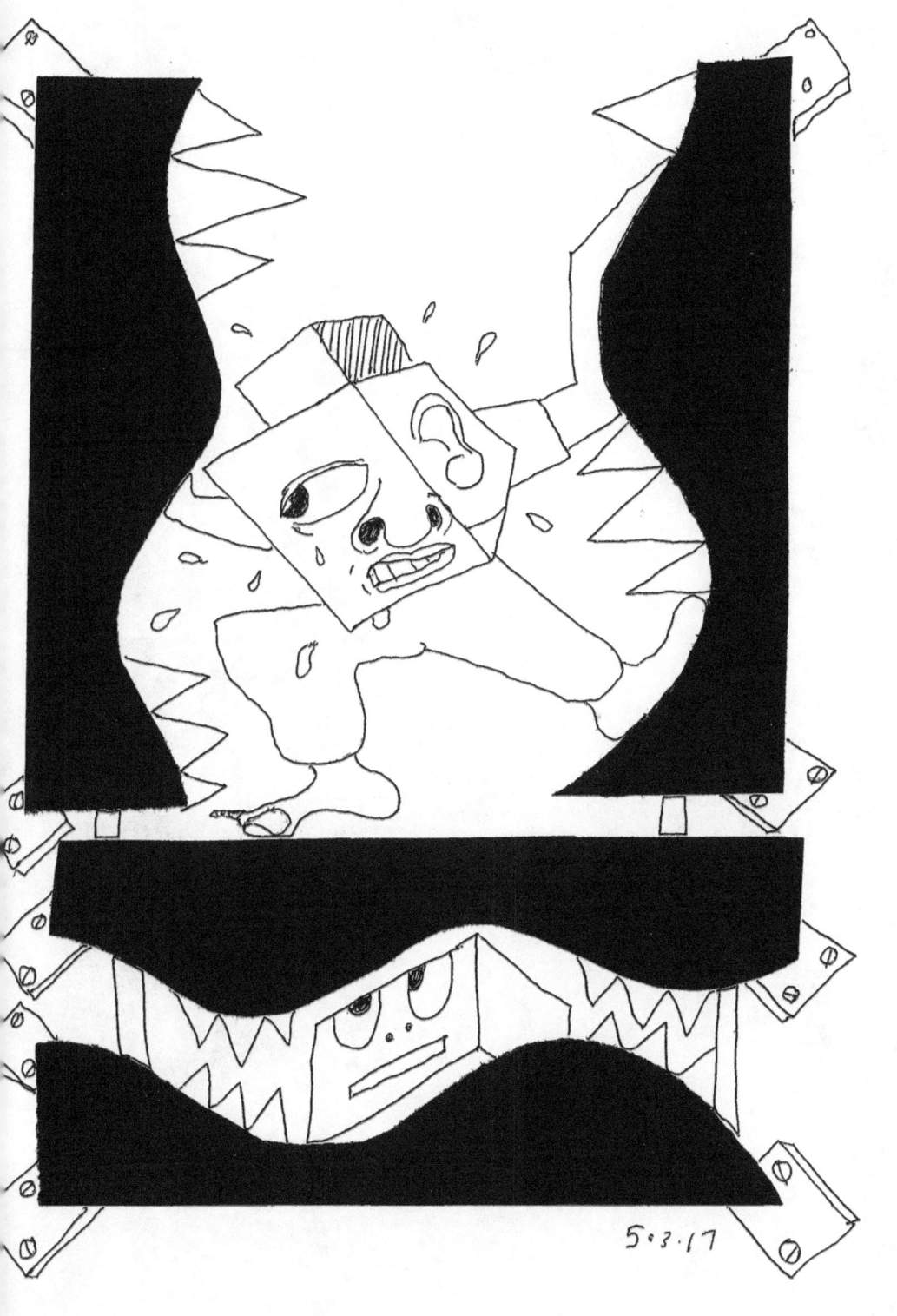

5·3·17

Sharing my gift with nothing

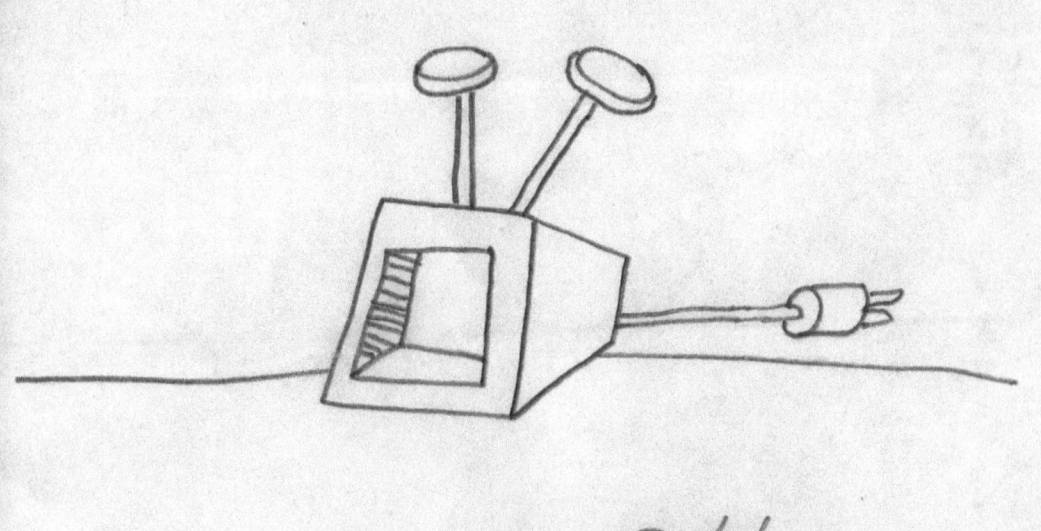

© 8/22/2017

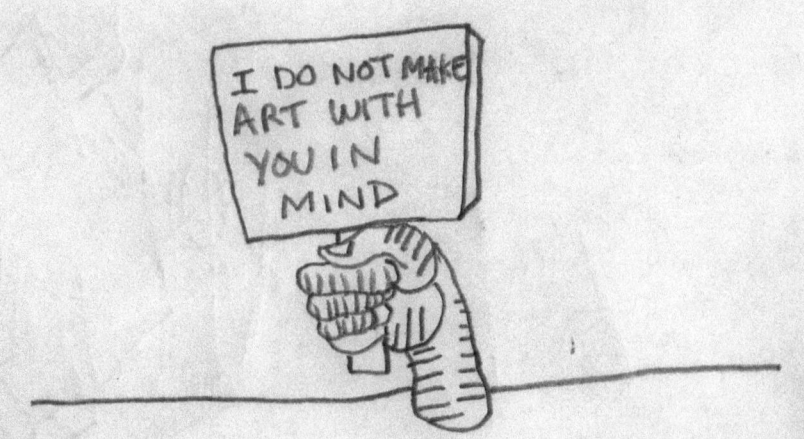

MARCellous Lovelace
© 8/22/17

It sounds like rain, dehydrated in the emptiness

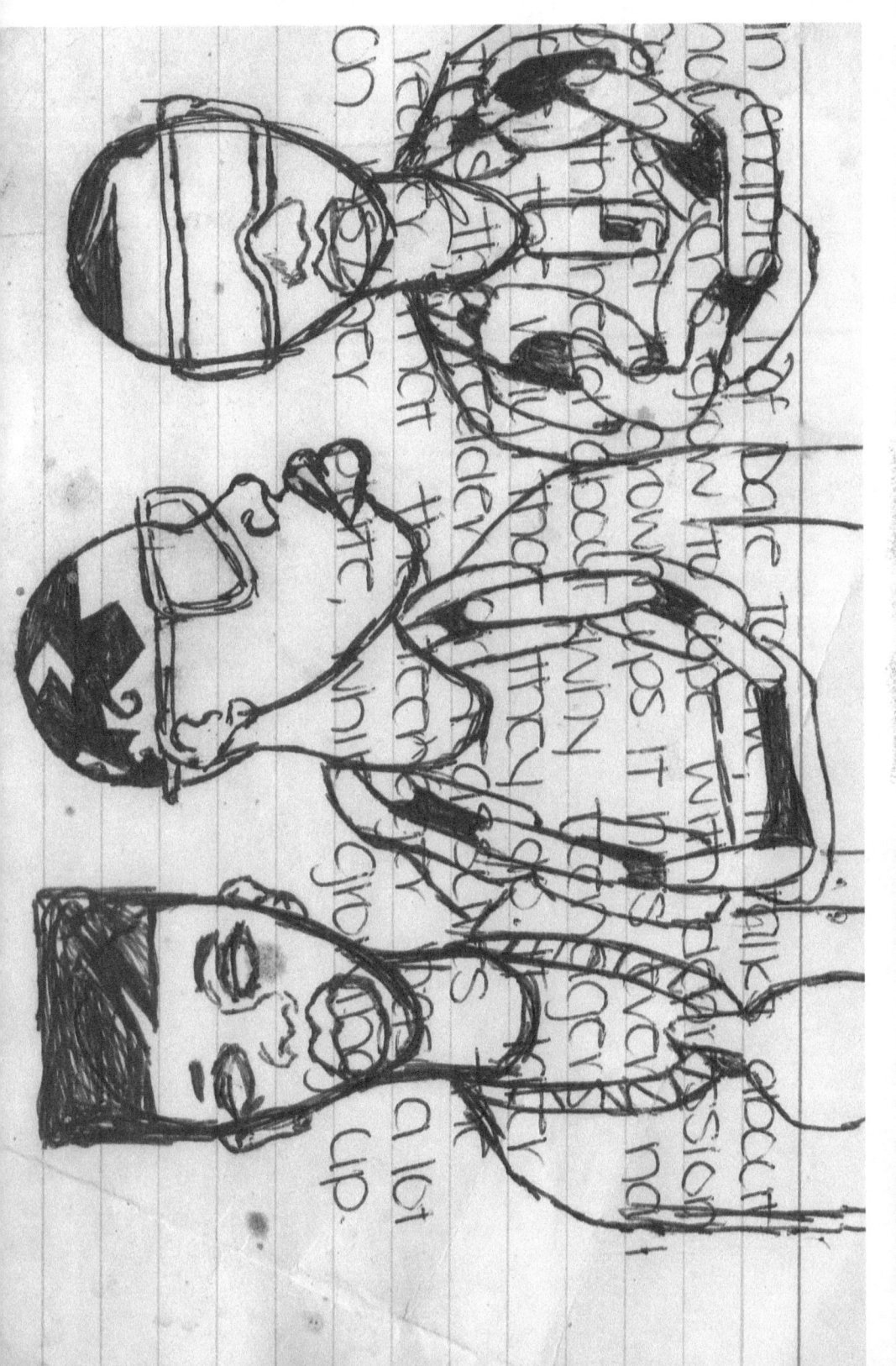

They wait to hear your voice

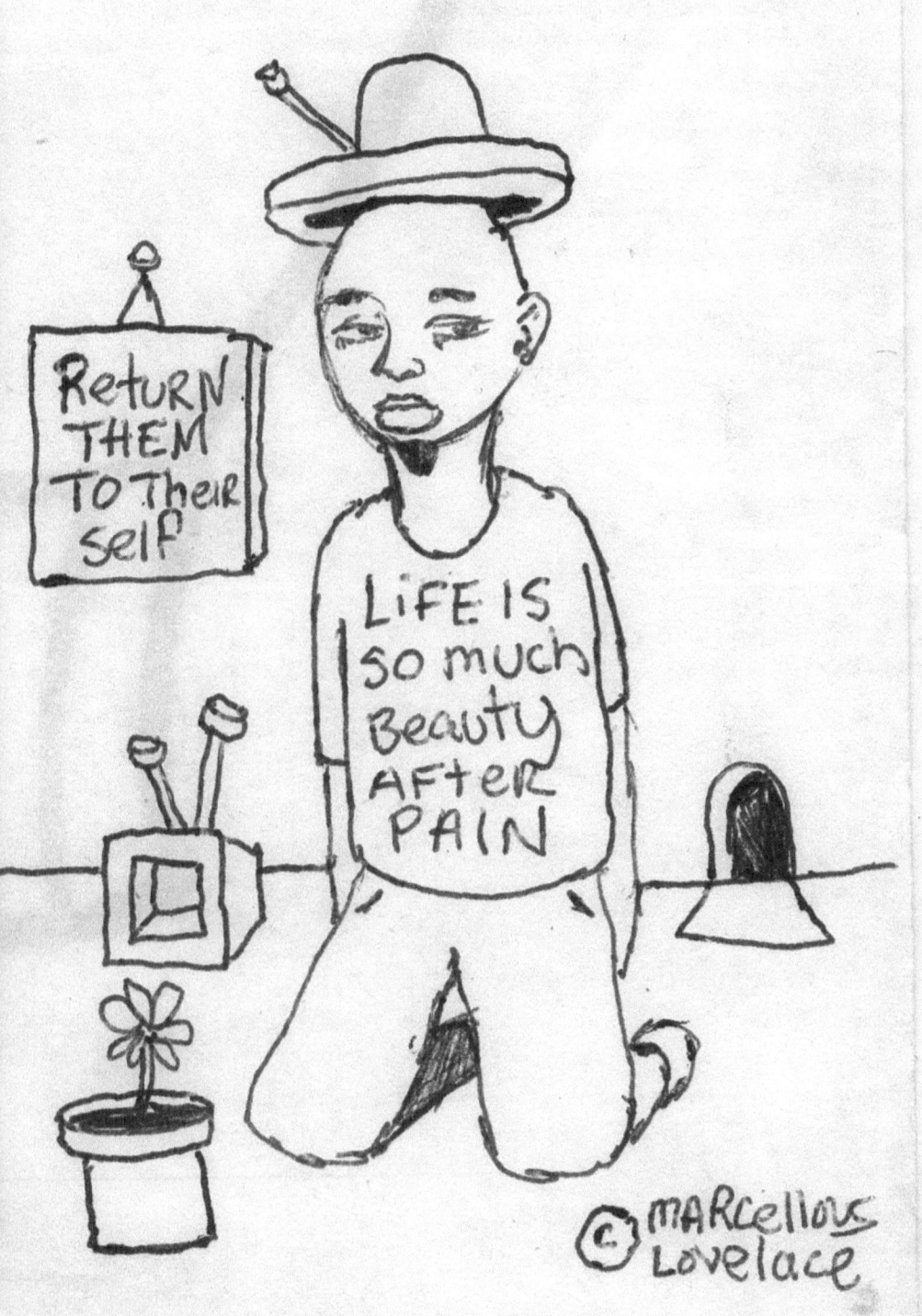

Taking my noise out of control

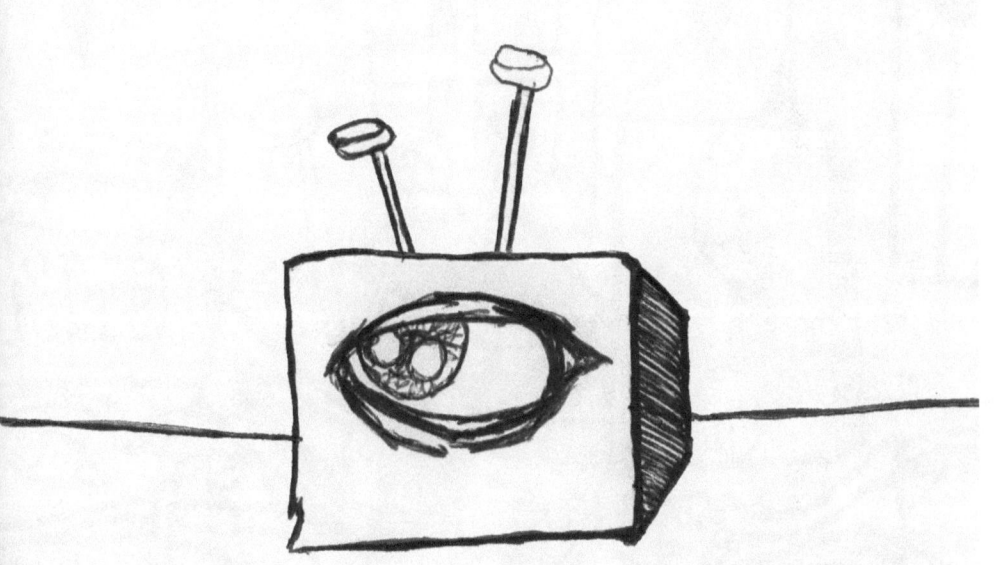

MARCellous Lovelace
©8/23/2017

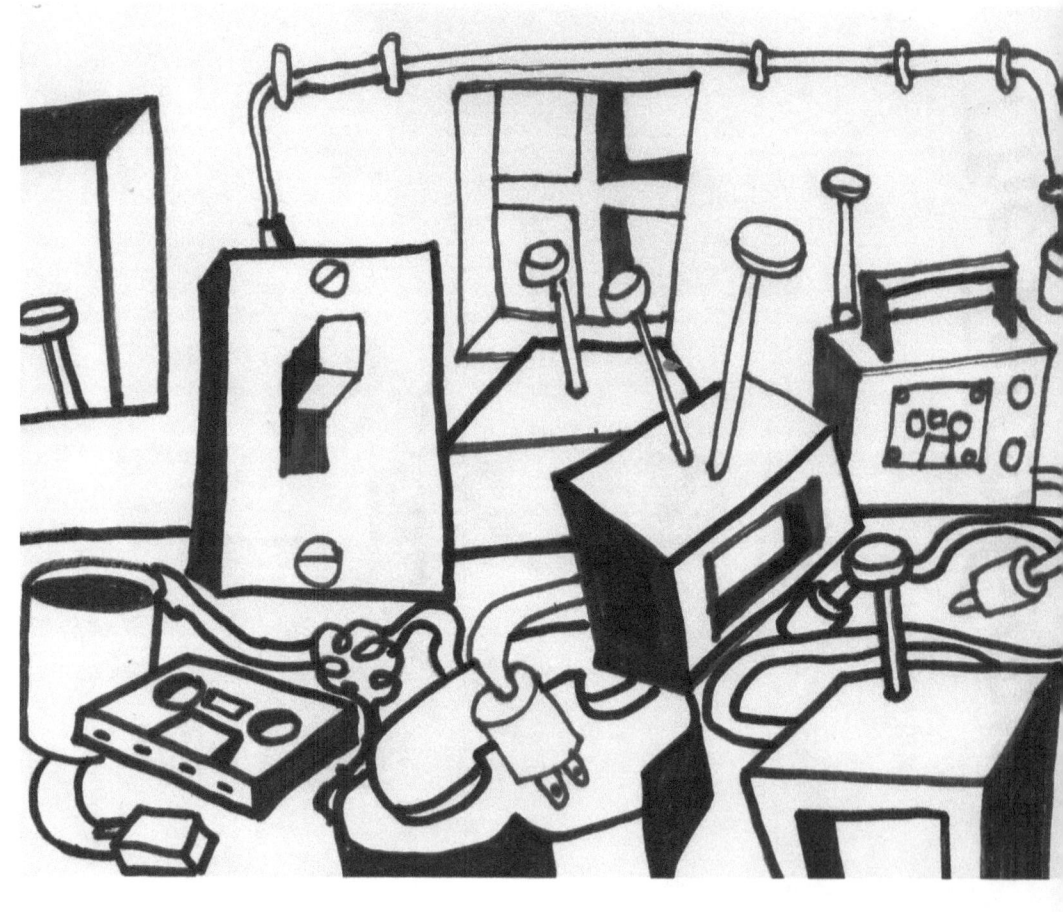

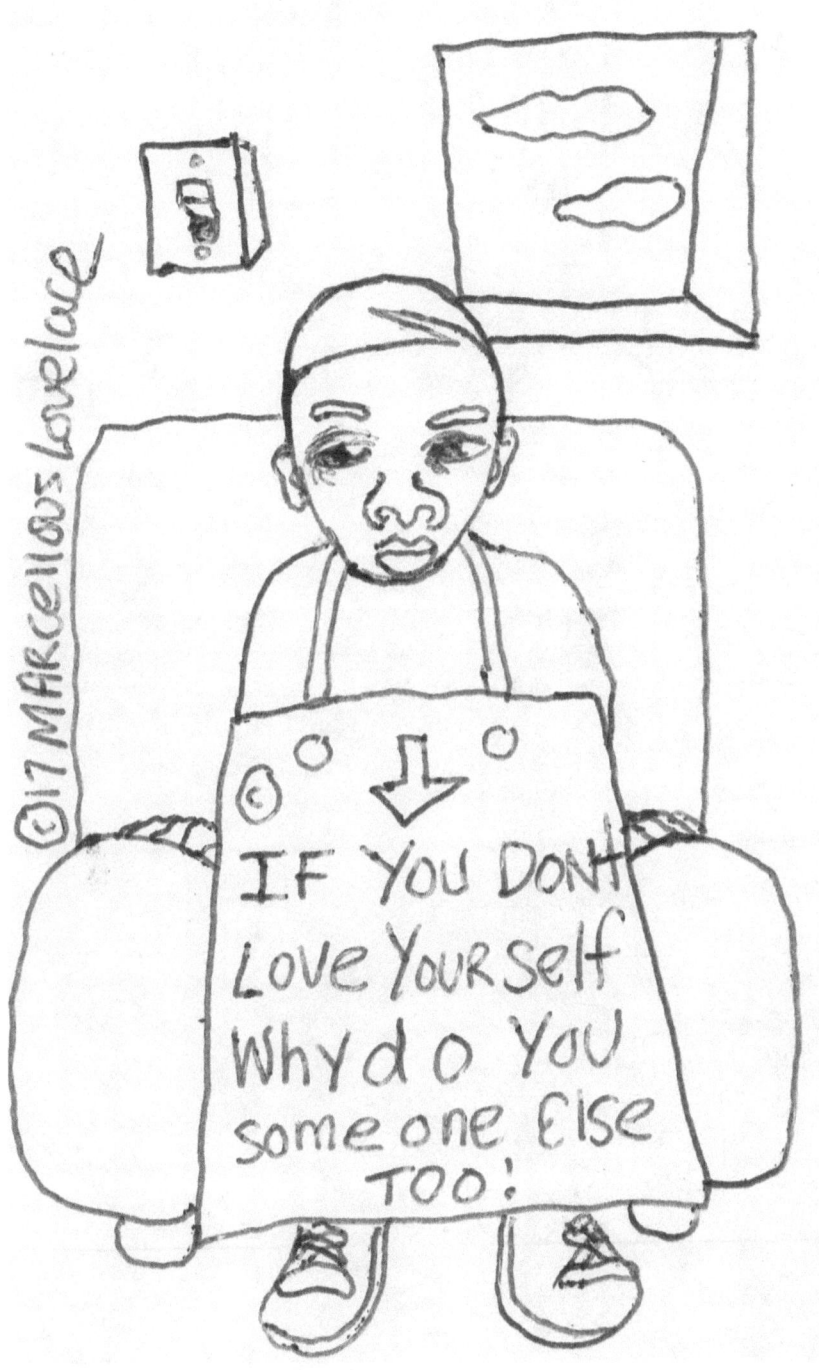

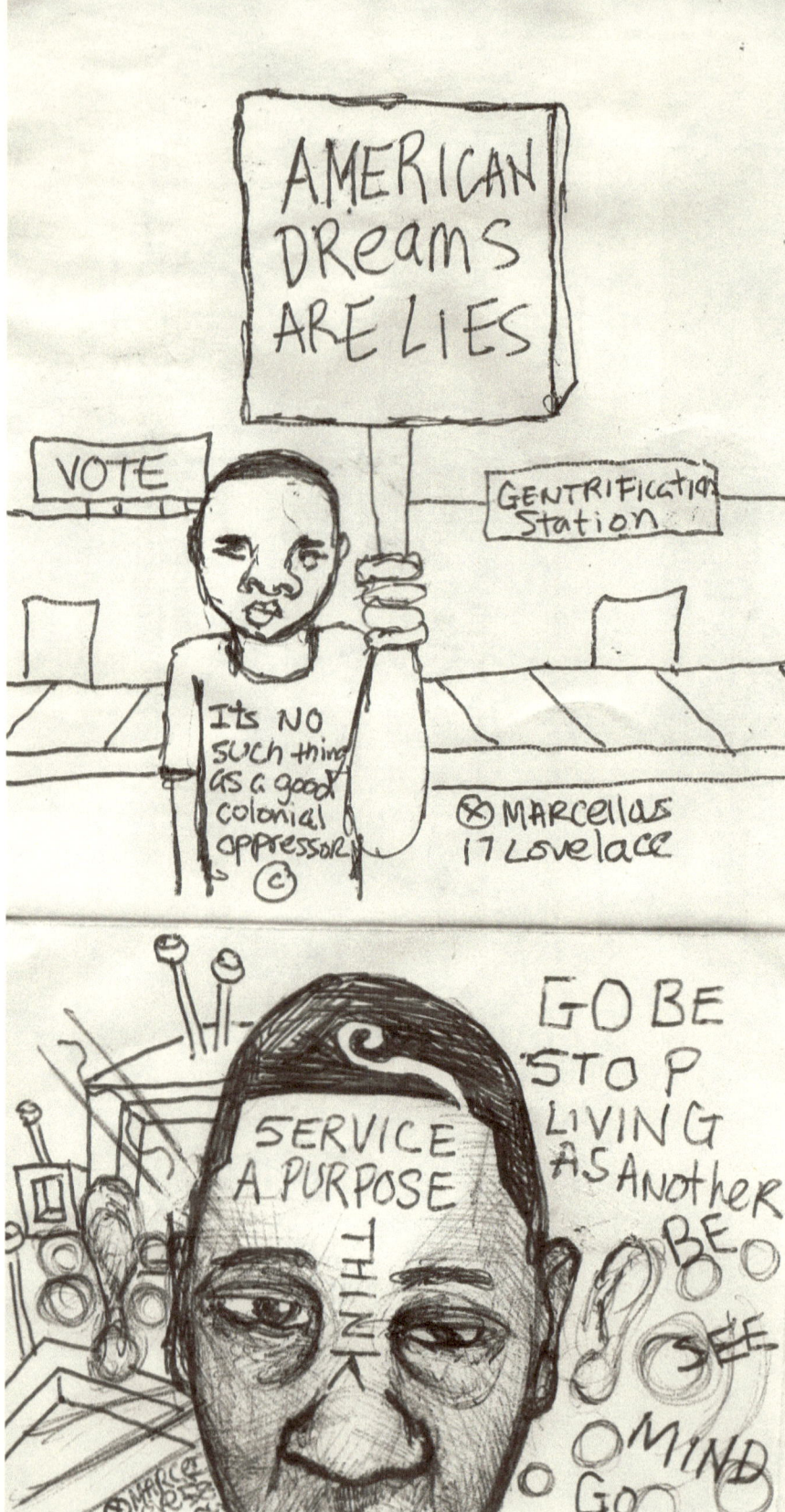

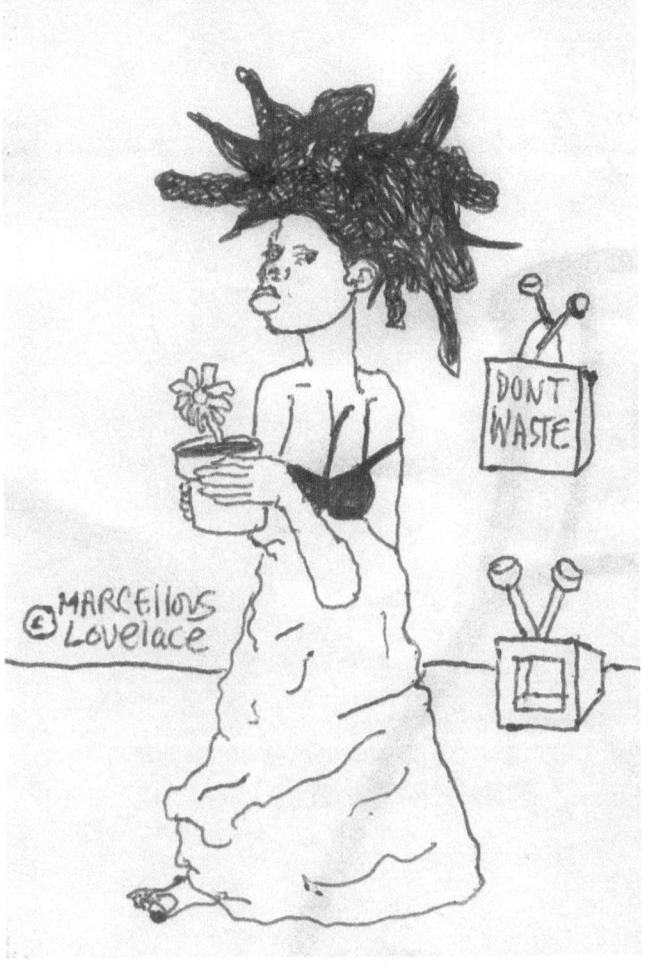

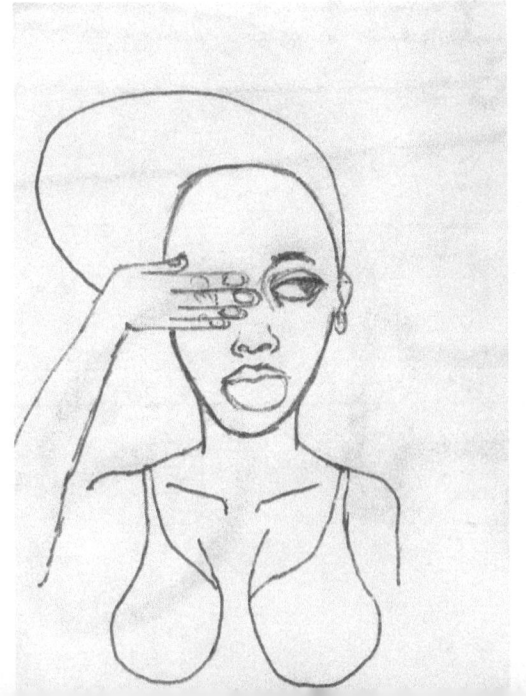

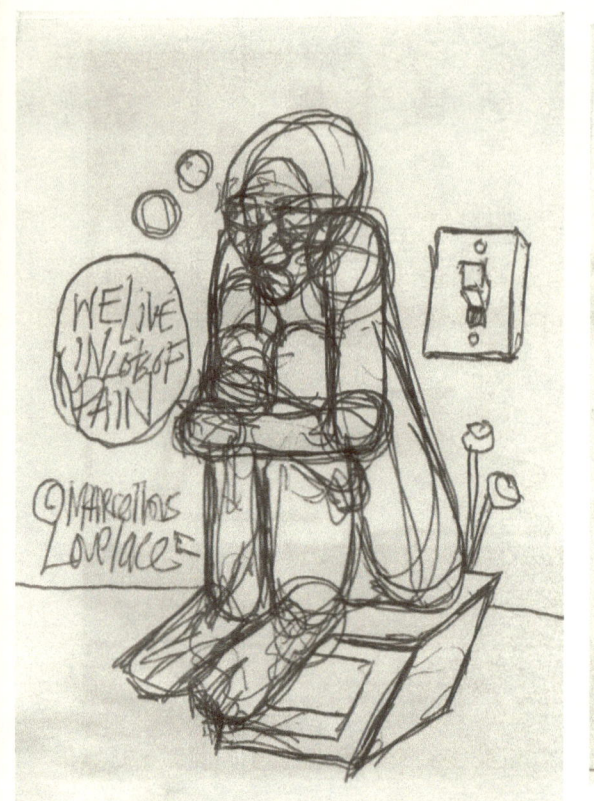

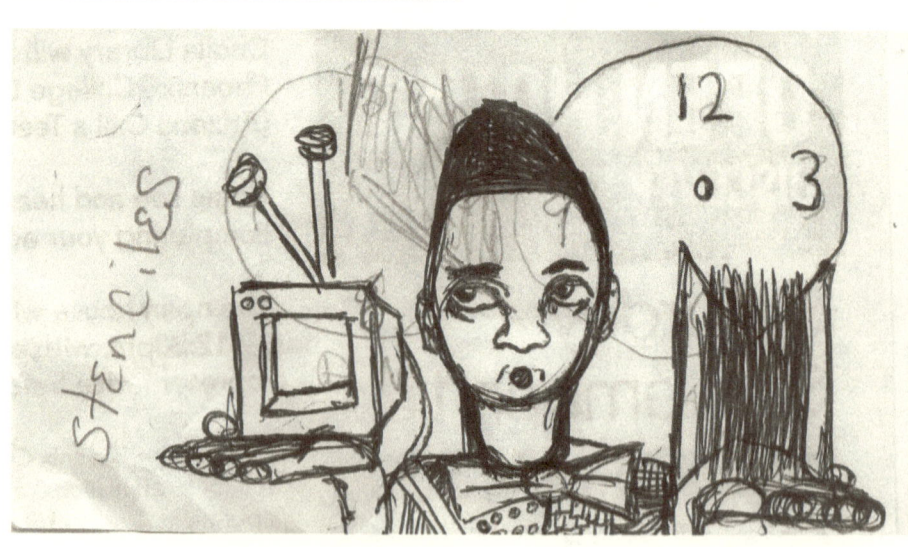

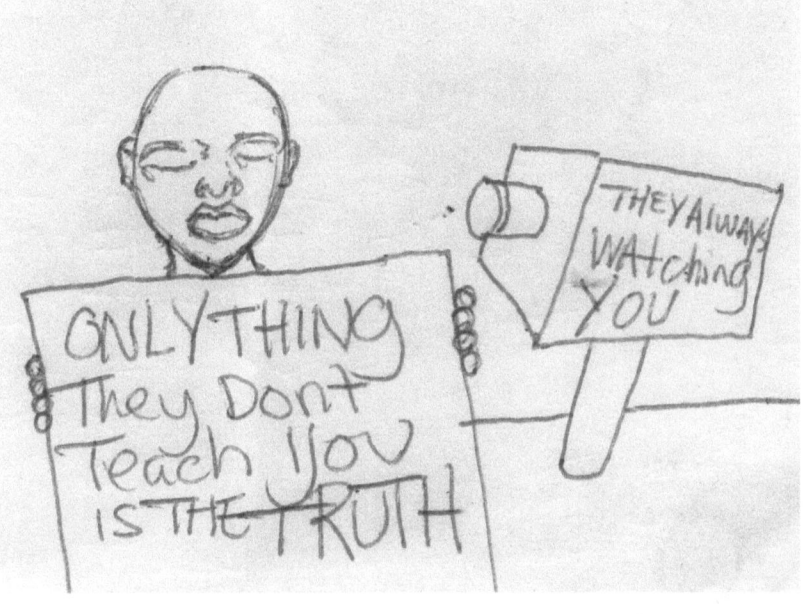

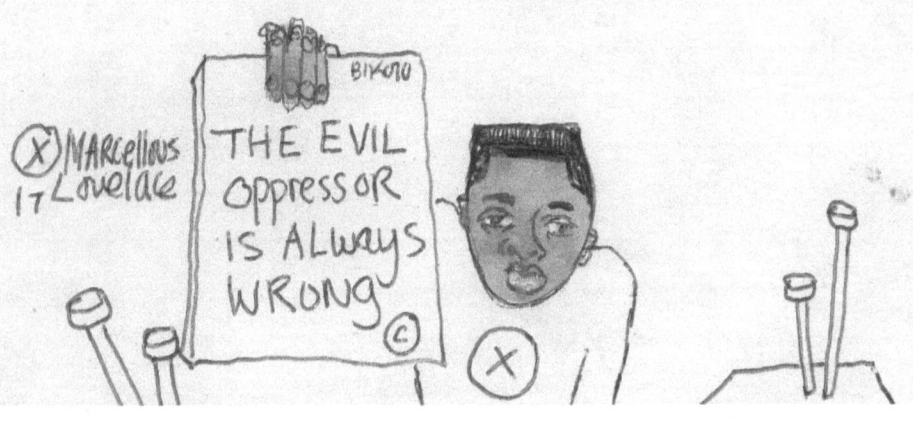

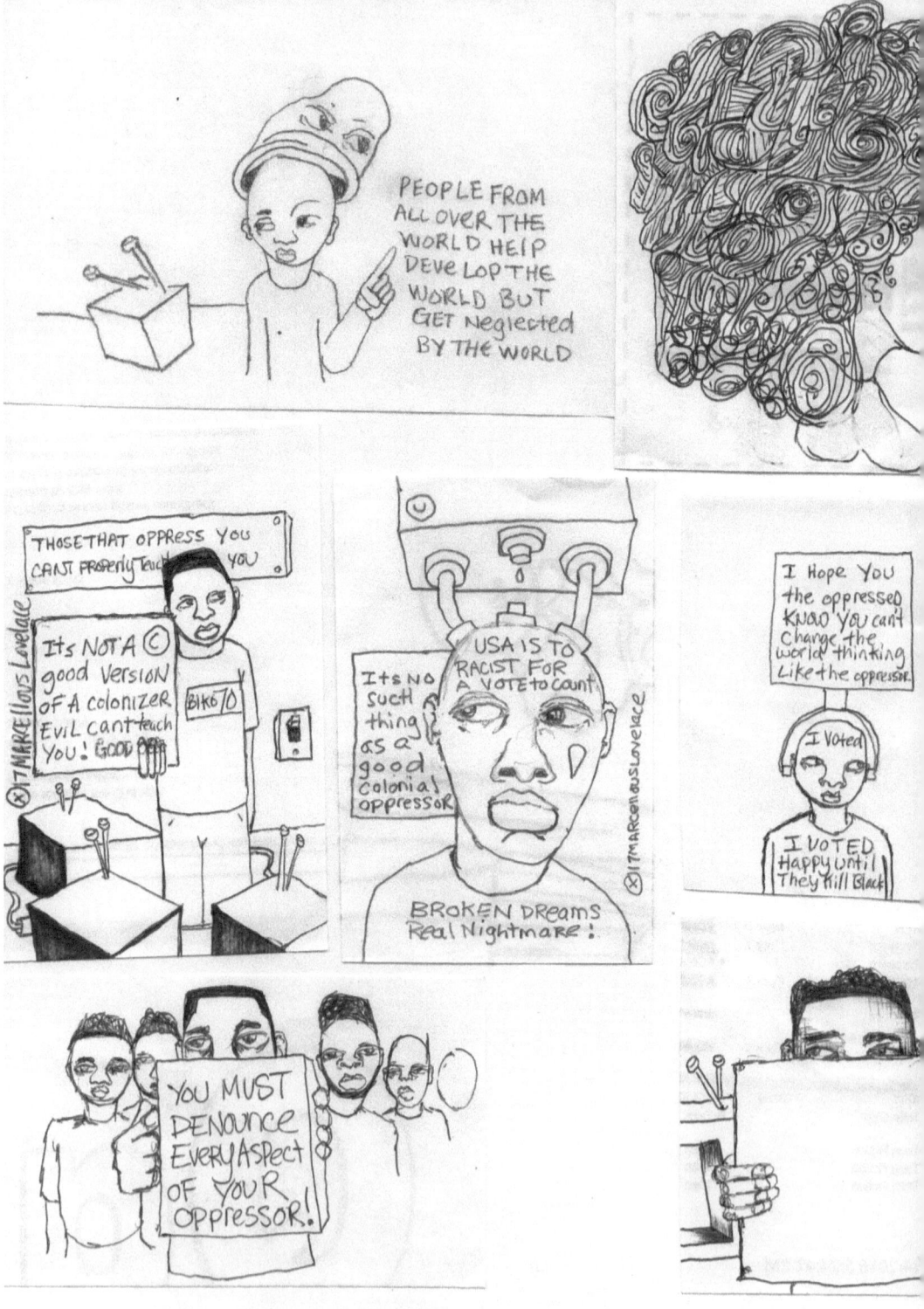

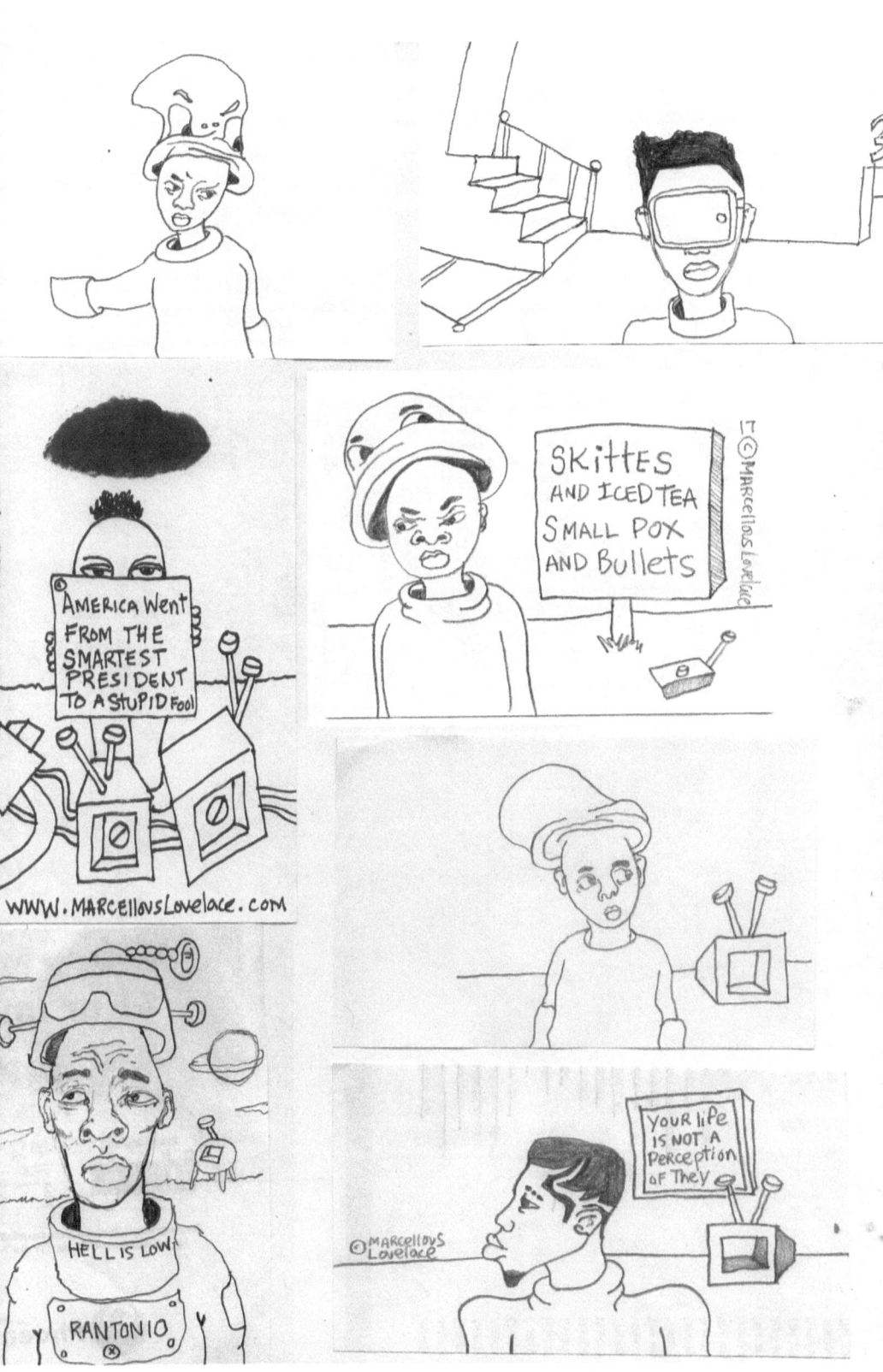

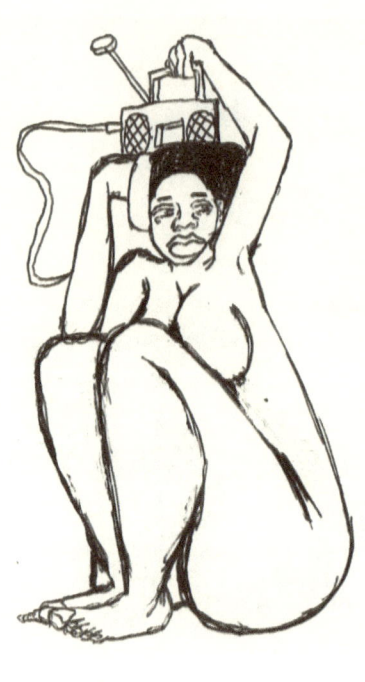

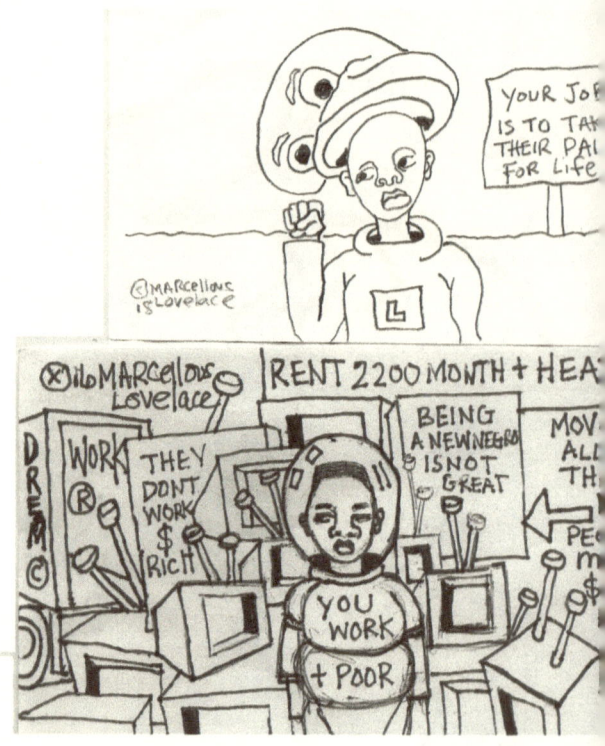

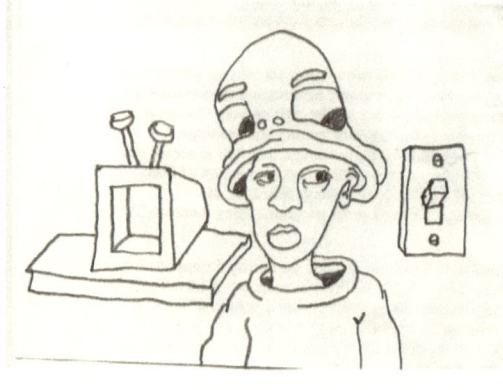

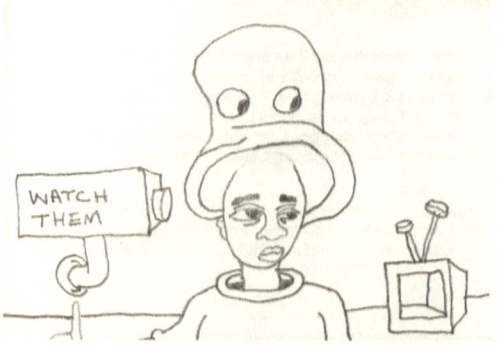

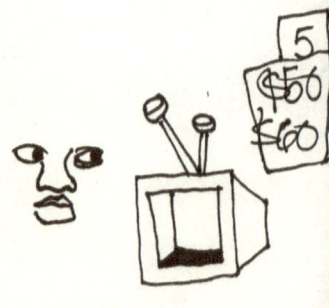

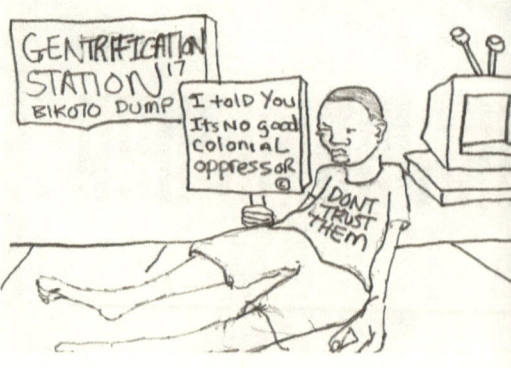

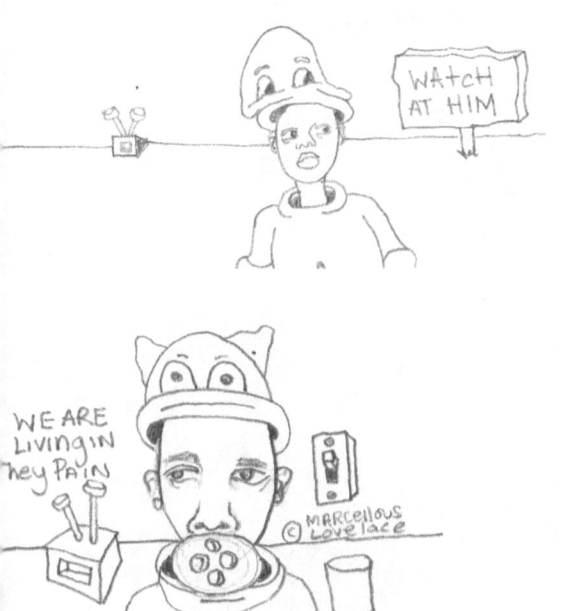
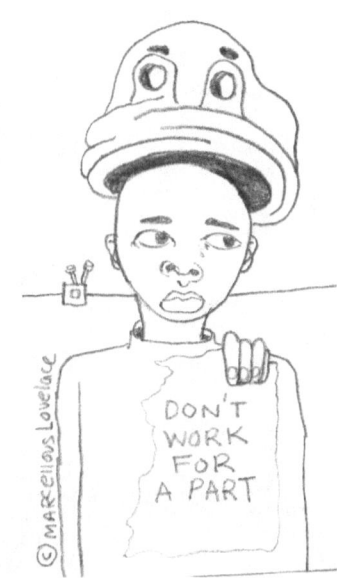
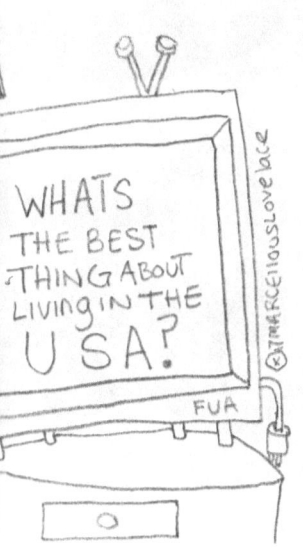
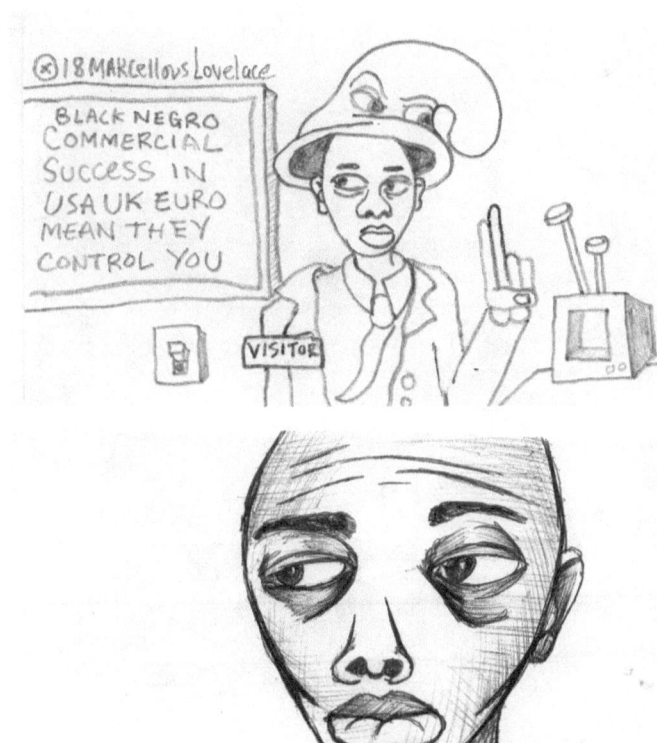

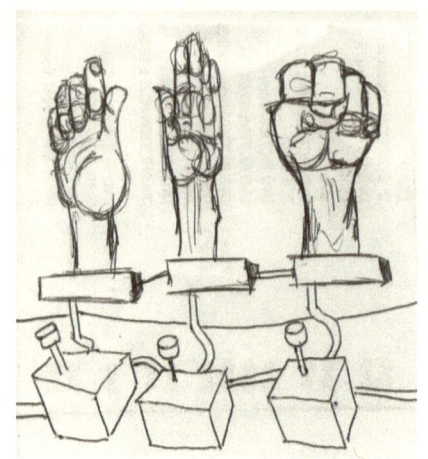

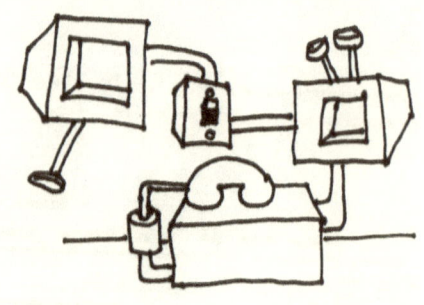

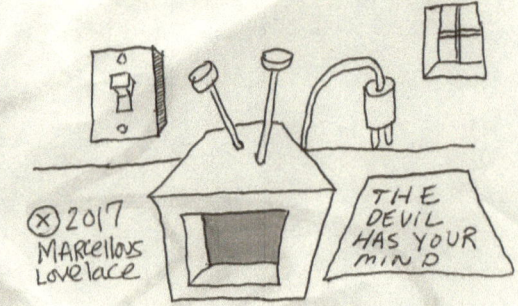

ⓧ 2017
MARCELLOUS
Lovelace

THE
DEVIL
HAS YOUR
MIND

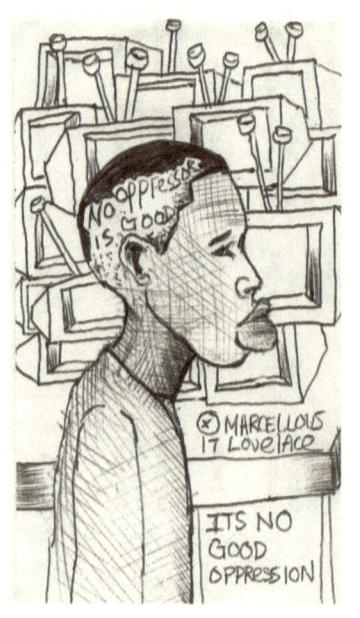

No oppression
is good

ⓧ MARCELLOUS
17 Lovelace

ITS NO
GOOD
OPPRESSION

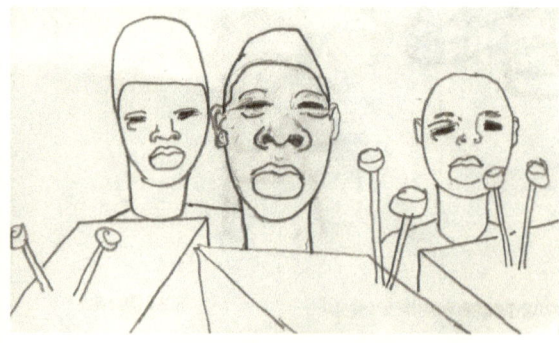

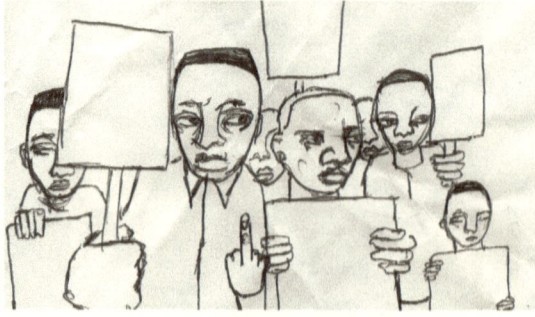

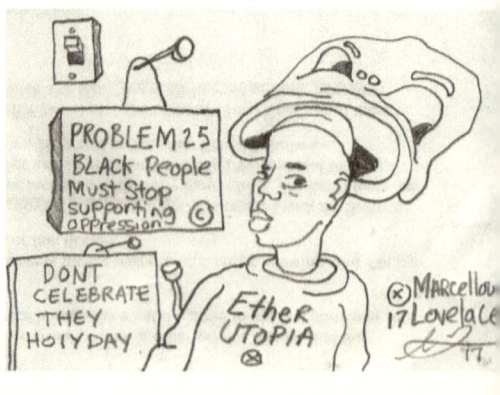

PROBLEM 25
BLACK People
Must Stop
Supporting
Oppression ©

DONT
CELEBRATE
THEY
HOLYDAY

Ether
UTOPIA

ⓧ MARcellous
17 Lovelace

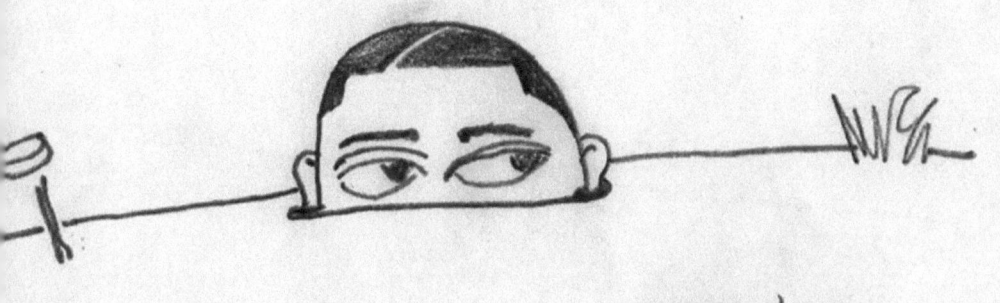

MARcellousLovelace
© 8/30/17

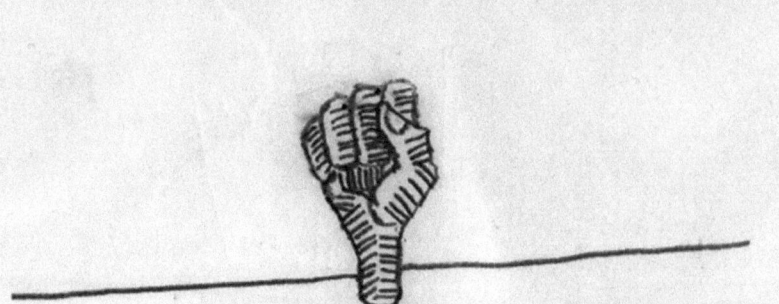

MARCELLOUSLovelace
© 8/22/17

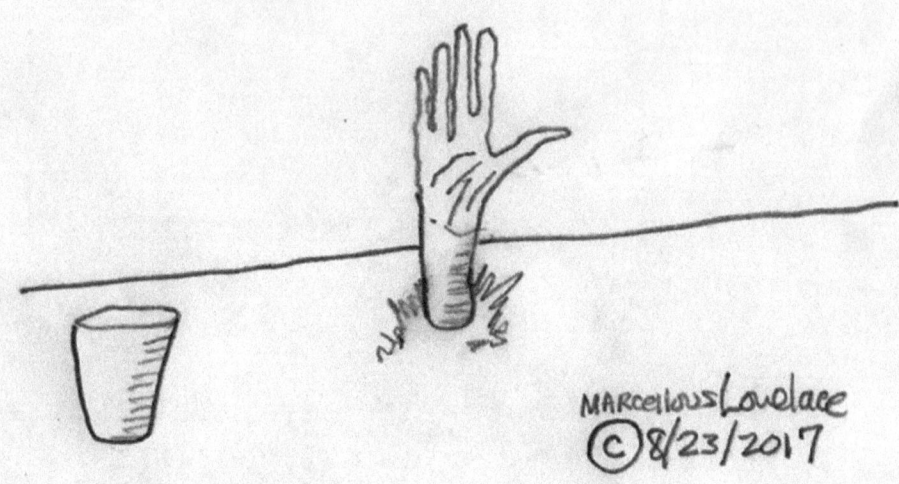

MARCEllous Lovelace
©8/23/2017

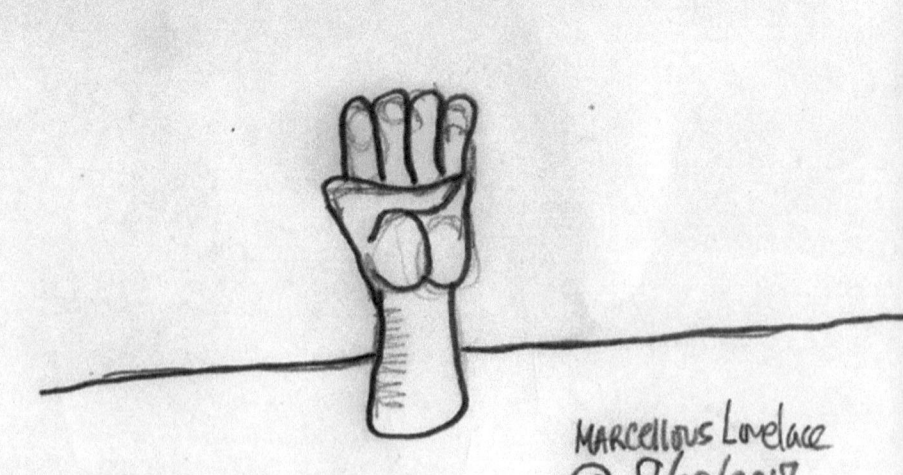

MARCEllous Lovelace
© 8/29/2017

www.ingramcontent.com/pod-product-compliance
Lightning Source LLC
Chambersburg PA
CBHW021924170526
45157CB00005B/2172